Ordinary Resilience

ORDINARY RESILIENCE

Rethinking How Effective Leaders Adapt and Thrive

LUIS VELASQUEZ

COPYRIGHT © 2024 LUIS VELASQUEZ
All rights reserved.

ORDINARY RESILIENCE
Rethinking How Effective Leaders Adapt and Thrive

FIRST EDITION

ISBN 978-1-5445-4564-6 *Hardcover*
978-1-5445-4563-9 *Paperback*
978-1-5445-4562-2 *Ebook*

To my wonderful wife, Rujeko, and our two smartass children, Alexis and Nathan

CONTENTS

INTRODUCTION 9

PART I: THE FOUNDATIONS OF RESILIENCE
1. THE RESILIENT YOU 19
2. *AMOR FATI* 51
3. PILLARS OF RESILIENCE 69

PART II: THE PILLARS OF RESILIENCE
4. EMBRACE THE SUCK 85
5. FACE YOUR FEARS 117
6. BUILD RELATIONSHIPS 147
7. FIND YOUR INNER STRENGTH 181
8. SOLVE FOR FULFILLMENT 209

CONCLUSION 225
ACKNOWLEDGMENTS 231
ABOUT THE AUTHOR 233

INTRODUCTION

"Why is the TV so loud?" my wife asked as she walked into the room.

"What do you mean?" I said. "It's not loud."

"My God, it's *so* loud!"

For months, Sara had been complaining that I was going deaf or that I was ignoring her. In reality, I wasn't exploring "selective auditory attention." I truly didn't hear what she was saying. The day with the TV was the last straw.

"Well, we need to do something," Sara continued. "We need to go see an ENT to check out your hearing. There is something wrong."

She made some calls, and a few days later, we visited an ear, nose, and throat doctor. He asked many questions and performed a few routine tests, including an auditory assessment that confirmed my hearing had been severely compromised, but he didn't know why. He asked us to go home and come back in a few months so he could check my hearing again and monitor the progress.

Thankfully, my wife didn't give in so easily. It was so clear to us that something was wrong that we had already done research on the possibilities. What might cause someone to lose their hearing so quickly—especially someone in their mid-thirties? Before visiting the doctor, we had gone through that list and scratched off the ones we knew didn't apply: exposure to sudden loud noises or a chronically noisy environment, a genetic condition, and an ear infection. The only possible cause left was a brain tumor. When the doctor told us to come back in a few months, my wife asked if it could be a tumor.

"It's possible," the doctor said, "but I don't think that's it. Brain tumors are rare. Let's just keep monitoring it."

"Can you order an MRI of his head?" she asked.

"I really don't think that's necessary," the doctor said. "Just come back in three months and we'll go from there."

My wife and I looked at each other uneasily, but stood up and started walking out anyway. As we reached the door, my wife hesitated. She looked back to the doctor and said, "No. You know what? We want an MRI. If you don't order it, we'll find someone who will."

Three days later, I was lying on the narrow table heading into the coffin-like environment of the MRI machine.

That evening, the phone rang just as I was heading out the door to go for a quick run. Oblivious to what was coming, I walked back to the half wall between the dining room and living room and answered it.

"Hi, Luis. Do you have a moment?" It was the doctor I had seen Tuesday morning. As quickly as I thought, *Why would he be calling me on a Friday at five?* I had the answer: "The MRI from this morning showed an unusual mass in your brain."

I have a perpetual smile on my face, but it immediately disappeared. My wife saw my reaction and rushed over to take the phone. She hit the speaker button and demanded to know what was going on. The doctor repeated the news and added that he had already booked an appointment with a neurosurgeon for the following week.

When we hung up, my wife collapsed by my side and started crying. Seeing her reaction was almost as hard as hearing the news itself. I felt numb, paralyzed with fear. Not only did I have a brain tumor, but it was clearly bad enough that the doctor had already scheduled a visit with a neurosurgeon. My thoughts were racing: *What am I going to tell my mom? How am I going to survive? Do I have the money to do this? Am I going to be buried here or in Guatemala? Will I die a horrible death?*

Sara and I talked until her tears slowed and then I decided to go for my run anyway. I needed to stop talking about it. I needed to clear my head and think.

As I ran, I thought. I thought about the lab where I worked. We dealt with a lot of radioactive material. I remembered the postdoc in my lab who was diagnosed with cancer and later passed away. He came to visit a few months before he died, and he was a shadow of the man I knew. I wondered if that was going to be my fate. I pictured myself looking sick, wasting away, and waiting for my death, and I was overcome with a deep sense of fear and helplessness. I also thought about my family in Guatemala—my mother, my dad, and my siblings—and how painful this news would be. As I ran, tears fell.

At that point in my life, I participated in 5Ks but I wouldn't call myself a runner. Five miles was the farthest I had ever gone. When I finally stopped running and crying that day, however, I had covered nine miles. My wife was so worried she was ready to call the police.

Something inside of me changed during those miles. I left the house full of fear and questions that I couldn't answer, but I returned filled with resolve. The situation hadn't changed. I still had a brain tumor, and I still had no idea what the future held. But I had accepted the worst possible outcome—that I might die from the tumor—and decided that in typical Luis fashion, I would go down fighting. I also asked myself one question: what am I going to do about this? Doing so allowed me to reframe the situation, see the possibilities, and start moving forward one step at a time.

That is the essence of resilience.

OUR PROBLEMS TO SOLVE

A brain tumor is an extreme example, but we all live through changes and challenges—a sick child, a car accident, a job loss. As a leader, you likely encounter difficulties related to missed promotions, toxic bosses, dysfunctional cultures, others' perceptions of how you show up, and more. If you are alive, you will encounter hard, distressing, and sometimes traumatic situations. Some will pass quickly, and some linger for what seems like an eternity.

No matter what the crisis, we tend to respond as I did during my run that day, focusing on the ifs and the perceived problems rather than on what is ours to solve.

We cannot control every variable, so focusing on the uncertainty only adds unnecessary anxiety and stress. We ruminate, overthink, try to find complex solutions, and wish we were in a different position to deal with what we face—but we're not even looking at the right problem to begin with. As a result, we struggle to move forward on the things that are actually within our control.

Think about my tumor: What could I do to change the fact that I had a mass in my brain? Nothing. What could I do to change the fact that I might die from that tumor? Nothing.

That tumor was my perceived problem—my *gravity* problem, as I call it. Gravity exists no matter what we do. We have absolutely no control over its presence. Likewise, many circumstances in life, like being diagnosed with a brain tumor, are outside of our control. In that sense, they are not our problems to solve.

What problems were for me to solve? The ones over which I could exert some control. I could take the next steps—see the neurosurgeon, have surgery, and make plans to rest during recovery. I could also control my reaction to the situation. On my run, I eventually decided that, whether I died of a brain tumor or old age, I was going down fighting. As long as I was alive, I was going to truly *live*.

In a sense, the outcome of any hurdle or ordeal isn't important. It's how you live through it that makes the difference. Resilience goes beyond merely coping or surviving or even bouncing back. It involves moving forward and thriving *because of* challenges, not in spite of them.

The good news is that resilience is not an extraordinary trait possessed by a special few; rather, it is quite ordinary and shared by everyone. Given that you already have what you need to adapt and thrive, the question is how much and how well you put it to use. This book will show you one way to unlock, develop, and exercise the resilience muscle you already possess.

A FRAMEWORK FOR RESILIENCE

As you've probably guessed, this book won't give you tips on changing your situation. In many cases, if not most, the situation won't change at all. I couldn't alter the fact that a brain tumor had formed, and I now live with the reality that it may return. Your boss may never change his abrasive style. You may not reach the C-suite in the next five years. Your coworkers may always see you as unapproachable and aloof.

However, you can change your reaction. You can learn to identify and solve for the problems that are truly yours to solve. You can move past the uncertainty and take the first step to adapt and eventually thrive. You already have what it takes.

The framework for resilience offered here is just that: a framework. It is not a blueprint. It is certainly not the only way to build the muscle that will help you deal with present and future obstacles. It has worked for me and the leaders I have coached, so I offer it to you.

In Part I, we discuss the first two aspects of the framework: *why* we should develop resilience and *how* we go about doing so through three key drivers—commitment, persistence, and optimism. We also discuss the concept of *amor fati*, "love of fate," and the importance of self-compassion in building your resilience muscle in four areas: mental, physical, spiritual, and social.

In Part II, we discuss the third aspect of the framework, the *what* of resilience development. Each chapter discusses one pillar of resilience, with suggestions for applying it in your leadership challenges. Each pillar has three key components and a motto to help you remember the essential truth:

1. *Embrace the Suck*: You can't control the rain, but you can choose whether or not you get wet.
    - *Accept* things as they are.
    - *Envision* the possibilities.
    - *Execute* the steps to realize your goal.
2. *Face Your Fears*: Don't aim to be fearless. Aim to fear less.
    - *Welcome* fear.

- *Challenge* your relationship with fear.
- *Act* because of fear.
3. *Build* Relationships: We cannot do life alone.
    - *Identify* the relationships you need to cultivate in your life.
    - *Evaluate* the perceptions others have of you and challenge your own perceptions.
    - *Engage* people with humility, assertiveness, and empathy.
4. *Find Your Inner Strength*: You are more capable than you think.
    - *Raise your standards* to set higher goals and expand your comfort zone.
    - *Understand your choices* between risk and safety.
    - *Take action* by using empowering rituals, habits, grit, and focus.
5. *Solve for Fulfillment*: Consider your contribution to the world.
    - *Find* your purpose.
    - *Live intentionally* according to your values.
    - *Recharge* to avoid burnout.

These pillars share one common denominator: practicing them requires you to take the first step. Execute, act, engage—all of these words imply movement or progress. Building resilience is a process; it requires action and it doesn't happen overnight.

To help you take the first step in these areas, each chapter includes specific action items, as well as examples from my coaching practice.

UNLOCK THE RESILIENCE WITHIN

Not every person flourishes in the face of change or challenge. Some people survive and merely function. Others recover or return to baseline. Then there are those who adapt and thrive as a result of a traumatic experience or undergoing change. The key to such post-traumatic growth is resilience.

My journey to writing this book started because I wanted to understand what resilience is. It has since shifted to understand not only what resilience is, but also what it takes to have it. In other words, what behaviors, attitudes, mindsets, and rituals help strengthen that muscle? This book answers that question and provides access to tools you can use to build your own resilience muscle.

In the context of leadership development, resilience is crucial to maximizing performance, reducing stress, and building collaboration and innovation. Resilience isn't a skill that can be coded into a person. You can't take a pill to become resilient. However, resilience can be coached and learned. It is a combination of attitudes, values, and behaviors that can be adopted, adapted, and cultivated over time. In truth, it's not a matter of learning to be resilient as much as it is learning to unlock the resilience within. Every leader has the ability to adapt and thrive.

To that end, we begin with a discussion of what resilience is—and isn't.

Part I

THE FOUNDATIONS OF RESILIENCE

Chapter 1

THE RESILIENT YOU

"The human capacity for burden is like bamboo—far more flexible than you'd ever believe at first glance."

—JODI PICOULT

- The essence of resilience
- The drivers of resilience
- What resilient leaders do
- What resilient leaders don't do

I come from a family of hard-working merchants. My great-grandfather emigrated from Italy to Guatemala and started a successful trading business. Like many wealthy immigrants of the day, he fathered a child out of wedlock—my grandfather—and left him to be raised in poverty by his mother. As a result, my grandfather didn't go to school or learn to read and write, but he had an affinity for numbers. He eventually started a business selling corn that slowly grew into one of the largest businesses in my hometown.

My father, the oldest child, began working for my grandfather when he was young. He didn't finish high school, as the demands of the family business—driving a truck all over the country to pick up goods to sell in my grandfather's store—took priority. Though my grandfather was a successful businessman, that didn't translate into providing more for his children, especially the older ones. When my parents met, my father was making the equivalent of twenty-five dollars a month. They soon married and moved into a small white adobe house with dirt floors, which is where they were living when I was born.

We were poor. When I was in elementary school, there were times when my mother, my siblings, and I shared one small meal. My mom sometimes fried corn tortillas, cut them up, and scrambled them with our eggs, and we would pretend we were eating meat since the mixture tasted like chicken. To have enough money to buy food, my mom occasionally pawned or sold wedding gifts she had received, and she also sewed dresses for people and charged two dollars apiece. I remember asking Dona Elena, a neighbor, for a small loan to buy our meal for the day. My mom always found a way to pay her back.

Though we didn't have material wealth, we had an abundance of laughter, learning, and love, which made for a very happy childhood. Our family grew to include two girls, in addition to my two brothers and me. My dad continued to work as a truck driver in my grandfather's business. He would be gone for days at a time, driving to different places in the country to pick up corn or sugar or whatever they needed to sell at the family store.

When I was fourteen, I won a scholarship to attend a boarding school in a town about six hours away. One night during my first year, I had a dream about blood. Oddly, I had dried blood in my nose the next morning. I forgot about it until four days later, when two of my aunts and their husbands came to see me. I was so happy because I never got visitors.

Soon, however, I realized something was terribly wrong.

My aunts told me that on Monday, the same day I had dreamed of blood and woken up with a bloody nose, my dad had been in a serious accident while driving his truck. Though my family had driven several hours to take me to see him in a hospital about five hours from my school, I still didn't grasp the seriousness of the situation.

When I arrived, I couldn't believe my eyes. My father's stomach was wrapped with bandages and both legs were suspended about twelve inches above the bed. He had ripped open his stomach, intestines, and bladder, and he had shattered both legs, one of which might need to be amputated. At that point, the doctors weren't sure whether he would survive. If he did, he wouldn't be the same person.

My hometown was about an hour from the hospital, and my mom made the gut-wrenching decision to send my brothers and sisters to live with different family members so she could care for my dad. Plus, with my dad not working, she couldn't afford to feed us. Mom often wondered aloud how we would survive this situation.

After the initial danger had passed, my dad was transferred to a hospital in the capital city. Six months later, he moved in with one of his sisters so he could be close enough to the hospital to receive the proper physical therapy. Little by little, he graduated to a wheelchair, and once he was more comfortable getting around, he moved back home.

From that moment on, my father became focused on one goal: starting his own business. He still couldn't stand, let alone walk, but he was already planning how to move forward. He wasn't merely looking for a way to survive or even to go back to work as a truck driver. He was determined to push beyond and thrive.

My mom and I were both skeptical, but he didn't let our doubts discourage him. "You'll see," he told us. "I'm going to buy a car and a house, and I'm going to send you to university, Luis." My mom entertained his dreams, but in secret she wondered, *If he didn't start a business when he was healthy, how could he do it in this condition?*

One day, my dad asked my grandfather if he could set up a table in his store, and my grandfather agreed. At first, my dad's business consisted of nothing more than a table, a scale, and a couple of knives. He would buy chicken meat and then cut, package, and sell it by the pound—all from his wheelchair.

As soon as my dad was able to, he dumped the wheelchair and started hobbling around on crutches—and he sold more and more chicken. He moved his table outside the front of the store, where he gained more visibility. Then my grandfather gave him a small room in his house with a door to the street, and my father opened his first shop.

When the volume increased to more than he and my mother could handle, my dad hired someone to help him with sales. Then a couple of restaurants asked him to provide chicken, and over time, my father became a very successful businessman. As a result, he was able to provide for our family in a way that we never thought possible. When I was eight years old, I had asked my dad for a bicycle, but he couldn't afford it. However, many years later when my little sister moved to the capital to go to the university, he had the resources to buy her a brand-new car.

Watching my dad adapt and thrive inspired a lot of people, my siblings and me most of all. All five of us have done very well as adults, in large part because of the example of resilience we saw in my dad. We have each encountered struggles and adversity, but among us we have a CFO and Senior VP for Citibank, an agricultural engineer, a dermatologist, a successful businessman, and an executive coach for leaders in Silicon Valley. Like my father, we all have what it takes to be resilient, and to inspire others to do the same.

As leaders, you are always creating impact. The question is, what type of impact do you want to create? In learning how to build your own resilience muscles, you will also positively influence others to do the same.

In this chapter, we'll look at what resilience is, the drivers required to develop it, and what it looks like in leaders.

THE ESSENCE OF RESILIENCE

The American Psychological Association defines resilience as the process of adapting in the face of adversity, tragedy, and significant sources of stress.[1] The key word is *adapting*, or making adjustments and modifications in behavior and thinking in order to effectively manage the challenge at hand.

Resilience is a well-researched subject, and there are a number of definitions and frameworks out there—some fancier than others, some much more academic and backed by research. With my clients, I use the following framework to discuss resilience development:

- *Why* work on resilience? To adapt and thrive
- *How* do we work on resilience? Through resilience drivers
- *What* tools can we use? Five resilience pillars

---

[1] American Psychological Association online dictionary, s.v. "Resilience," updated April 19, 2018, https://dictionary.apa.org/resilience.

We'll start by exploring the *why* and look at different aspects of adapting and thriving; then we'll discuss the *how*. The *what* is covered in Part II.

MORE THAN JUST SURVIVING

When people face adversity, they ideally go through three stages. First, they survive the incident, which often feels like an accomplishment in itself. Second, they adapt to the incident so it no longer affects them every day. Finally, they thrive as a result of what they've gone through.

The problem is that many people get stuck in survival mode and never move on to thriving.

Resilience is more than just continuing to exist despite a bad situation. People who remain in abusive relationships or cope with toxic bosses are sometimes seen as resilient because they endure the situation day after day. That's not resilience. That's surviving. Resilience involves adapting and then growing and developing to the point of prospering and flourishing.

When we are merely surviving, there is little room to dream, to envision a different future, to think beyond the current hardship. Whether the situation is traumatic or a more mundane work struggle, when we are in survival mode, we can't see the possibilities that lie beyond what's right in front of us. We're only able to figure out the next thing, and then the next thing. Survival mode is a natural defense mechanism to keep ourselves going, but it doesn't leave room for truly adapting and moving in a different direction.

If you find yourself in survival mode, stop for five minutes and picture what the future could hold. Taking time to dream allows you to have a destiny beyond your current challenge. It also allows you to start thinking about how you can use what you presently have to get there, which is a key part of the next stage: adapting.

Someone who has moved beyond survival mode is able to look at the difficult situation and take actions, however small, to make it not just livable, but better.

Marcus Aurelius once said, "The impediment to action advances action. What stands in the way becomes the way."[2] The challenge you experience may not be something you can change. I couldn't alter the fact that I had a brain tumor. You may not be able to stop the company reorg that will effectively block your promotion. However, you can turn that negative situation into something positive that gives you meaning and purpose. Once you grasp this perspective, you've moved into the last stage of resilience: thriving.

The person in survival mode sees the problem as something to put up with. The person who is in adapting mode sees the problem as something to be fixed. The person in thriving mode sees the problem as an opportunity to make a change and contribute meaningfully to the lives of others in the process.

NOT A QUICK FIX

Humans have been adapting for thousands of years. In fact, we are the most adaptive species on planet Earth. Whereas animals have survival superpowers such as sharp claws, incredible speed, and big, venomous fangs, humans have an incredible adaptive capacity. In a physical sense, we are the weakest species, yet we are dominant because we have been able to adjust to stressors—animal, human, and environmental alike.

---

[2] Marcus Aurelius, *Meditations* 5.20, from *The Thoughts of the Emperor M. Aurelius Antonius*, trans. George Long (1862), https://lexundria.com/m_aur_med/5.20/lg.

The problem is that we humans forget we have this adaptive capacity. As a result, when faced with challenges or trauma, our first response is often to look outside ourselves for a quick fix. Resilience, however, is not a quick fix.

If a person has high blood pressure, for example, the Band-Aid solution is to take medication to lower their blood pressure. An adaptive response, however, would be to alter their lifestyle: start eating healthy, begin an exercise program, lower stress, and so on. Both responses resolve the issue, but only the latter brings long-lasting, transformative change.

Let's say John is a neurosurgeon doing fantastic work in a certain hospital. He moves to a different hospital with expectations of performing at the same level but finds that is not the case. He knows he's a good surgeon and can't figure out what's going on.

To quickly rectify the situation, John tries a strategy that brought excellent results at his old job. He tries that strategy over and over, but like trying to fix high blood pressure with medication, only some progress is made. It doesn't get to the root issue or bring lasting change. He needs to dig deeper.

In John's case, his success at the former hospital may have partly resulted from his well-oiled team. If he doesn't have the same cohesive group in his new position, that will likely affect his performance. To get to a real solution, John has to look at what he's dealing with now. For example, if his performance issues are linked to a disjointed team, he might need to figure out how to show up differently to create more cohesiveness. An adaptive change is a change of mindset, not just behavior.

To navigate challenges at work and beyond with more than just a "one pill" approach, we need to tap into that innate adaptive capacity. We need to look beyond what has worked in the past and consider what the underlying issue might be right now. This takes time and intentionality.

REQUIRES DELIBERATE PRACTICE

One of my biggest passions is long-distance running. Prior to 2003 when I was diagnosed with a brain tumor, the farthest I had ever run was five miles. Compare that with 2008, when I ran thirty-six marathons—in one year!

That endurance level didn't happen overnight. It took a lot of practice, and it involved a lot of injuries. For a very long time, I trained somewhat mindlessly. Like our fictional neurosurgeon John, I kept following the same plan and technique, without bothering to find out if I was actually running correctly. My goal was simply to log miles, as if the more I ran, the better runner I was going to become. Instead, I kept getting injured. Around 2009, when I was recovering from one of these injuries, I finally researched the best way to run, and I took deliberate steps to fix my running form. And guess what? After that, I stopped experiencing running injuries.

No matter what the challenge, we develop resilience when we are intentional about learning what works and what doesn't. It involves being more objective about our situation, and not so emotionally attached to the old ways and mindset. Even if what we're doing is not working, we often stick with the plan because it's known and comfortable. Resilience requires deliberate choices to develop new skills, practice new techniques, and become comfortable with being uncomfortable.

REQUIRES GRIT

In her book *Grit: The Power of Passion and Perseverance*, Angela Duckworth uses West Point cadets as an example of individuals who display grit—the ability to suffer, be uncomfortable, and withstand pain because they are focused on a long-term aspirational goal.

No matter what the situation, the ability to withstand suffering is driven by the light at the end of the tunnel. For my dad, the light was owning his own business. For you, it might be becoming an entrepreneur, revolutionizing your industry, or becoming CEO. Having an aspirational goal makes it possible to endure the struggle because you have hope that your effort will pay off someday.

To help my clients step out of their comfort zone and develop grit, I guide them toward focusing on the light at the end of the tunnel *and* the steps they can take right now to get there. I often ask, "What can you do today so that in three years, you can say that this crisis is the best thing that could have happened to your career, your life, your business…?" Envisioning a different future strengthens the resolve to get through the discomfort now.

For some of us, moving outside our comfort zone feels very risky. But if you think of it as a means of growth, the risks feel more palatable. Moving your boundary will still feel uncomfortable and may even cause suffering, but that's how you adapt and grow.

IS A DISH BETTER SERVED COLD

Resilience requires grit, but developing it doesn't require a life full of traumatic experiences. You can increase your tolerance to discomfort by intentionally putting yourself in uncomfortable positions to learn to persevere amid pain. Just know that the time to put yourself in these mini resilience-building experiences is *not* when you're in the midst of a crisis. Like revenge, resilience is a dish better served cold.

At one point in my life, I had trouble accepting rejection. My inability to do so compromised my livelihood. As a solopreneur, I have to constantly put myself out there in pursuit of business, but the fear of rejection paralyzed me to the point of inaction. After reading Jia Jiang's blog post "100 Days of Rejection Therapy," I was inspired to proactively build resilience by putting myself in situations where I knew I would be rejected.[3] For example, I went to a McDonald's drive-thru and asked for a refill on a hamburger. With each small rejection, I became a little more comfortable with all rejection.

One of the resilience pillars we'll discuss in Part II is building relationships. I regularly engage in one-minute acts of kindness such as writing a short recommendation on a LinkedIn profile for someone who hasn't asked for it. That small act strengthens my relationships and builds my social resilience muscles, which will help when the need arises.

To develop grit, I create physical challenges for myself. For example, before I step out of a hot shower, I turn the water all the way to cold and let the water shock me. I'll also do two hundred push-ups a day for a month or one thousand sit-ups over the course of a weekend. This is not only good for my body, but it gives me small opportunities to endure pain and build physical resilience and build my adaptive capacity. These resilience-building practices will come in handy to build your adaptive capacity.

While COVID-19 was still going strong, companies were already discussing ways to prepare for the next time they have to endure large-scale changes and adaptations. Although this is wise, organizations and individuals don't need a pandemic to prepare for the next challenge. In fact, a crisis is not the time to prepare at all; that's when you should be able to exercise the

---

[3] Jia Jang, "100 Days of Rejection Therapy," *Rejection Therapy with Jia Jang* (blog), https://www.rejectiontherapy.com/100-days-of-rejection-therapy.

muscles you've already built. Instead, we can be intentional about building mental and physical strength, learning to suffer, and learning to adapt and thrive when the struggle is "cold" so we're ready the next time s*** hits the fan.

THE DRIVERS OF RESILIENCE

How do we go about developing this gritty capacity to adapt and thrive? Based on my experience, my dad's, and that of the leaders I coach, I believe there are three drivers that lead to resilience:

- *Commitment*: dedication, allegiance, or devotion to an idea, aspirational goal, value, or person
- *Persistence*: the ability to keep moving forward despite the pain and discomfort
- *Optimism*: hope and confidence in success for the future

Working together, these drivers provide a formula for adapting and thriving in the face of adversity, with optimism multiplying the positive effects of commitment and persistence:

(commitment + persistence) × optimism = resilience

Commitment and persistence alone are not enough. With zero optimism, you have zero resilience.

For as long as I can remember, my dad has been *committed* to providing for his family. Though he often thought about starting his own business when I was growing up, for various reasons he kept his commitment by working for my grandfather rather than by following his dreams.

When my dad lost the use of his legs following the accident, however, he experienced a mental shift that propelled him to act. He knew it wouldn't be easy—physically painful recovery, being confined to a wheelchair and then learning to stand and walk, starting a business with very few resources—but by adding *persistence* to his commitment, he started moving in the right direction, one chicken sale at a time.

Though my mom and I were skeptical, my dad had no doubt he would achieve his goal. He had always been a dreamer, but optimism alone hadn't been enough for him to push through the challenges associated with starting a business. Paired with his commitment and persistence, however, my dad's optimism multiplied the effects of the first two drivers and provided the north star, the guiding light, that allowed him to push through the hardship of his accident and become a successful businessman.

Possessing one of these drivers is not enough to adapt and thrive in life's adversities; the three must work together. Some leaders are committed to receiving feedback and honing their skills. When they are passed over for a promotion or receive specific suggestions for improvement, however, they need more than commitment to keep going; they need the ability to persist through pain and discomfort. Some leaders are dreamers, but like my dad, they need more than optimism to overcome the obstacles that are sure to come along. It is the formula of (commitment + persistence) × optimism that allows us to build ordinary resilience.

At the same time, it's possible to be persistent in keeping a commitment that ultimately proves harmful. My client Kimberly was committed to doing her job excellently and thoroughly, no matter what was asked of her. She persisted through the stress and late hours that came with finishing the numerous tasks dumped on her plate, but she was getting burned out. Because she was so good at her job, management decided they would need to hire three people to do what she was currently doing. At the same time, management was under the perception that Kimberly's potential had reached its limit, so she was stuck between being good at her job and not good enough to be promoted.

Through our coaching sessions, we determined that what Kimberly really wanted was to add value to her organization and to grow as a leader—not simply complete the work and do her job. Once she shifted her commitment to what she wanted, her persistence and her optimism about succeeding propelled her to take different actions that led to a more productive outcome. She started highlighting her potential and taking steps to delegate and elevate her direct reports so they could step up to the plate and Kimberly could spend her time in more strategic endeavors.

If we are like Kimberly, persistently doing work without a defined goal, we're living in survival mode, doing the same thing over and over but ultimately just existing in the same place. There's no room for considering a different outcome. As mentioned, resilience is more than just surviving; it's adapting, growing, and flourishing. In the context of resilience, having a strong commitment to the appropriate goal leads to greater persistence to see the outcome happen. Persistence in itself is an advantageous quality because it has positive unintended consequences. For example, my dad wanted to provide for his family by starting a business selling chicken, and through persistence in pursuing that dream, he not only succeeded in building a business, but he became an expert in his field. In addition, persistence over time shows ambition, a value for hard work, and consistency, all desirable characteristics in the workforce.

In producing these outcomes, intended and not, persistence is only as good as its connection with commitment and optimism. In survival mode, some people are incredibly persistent, but that's where it ends. There's no dreaming about the future, because there is no room to dream. There is no room to view the hardship as an opportunity to learn and grow. And there is no resilience.

While commitment is the mental devotion to achieving a goal and persistence is consistently doing the work necessary to get there, optimism is the hope and confidence that you will succeed, no matter the current situation. Optimism involves three key factors:

- A growth mindset that enables you to see setbacks as opportunities for learning
- A positive outlook about yourself, others, and the situation
- The ability to accept responsibility for mistakes without dwelling on them

Being optimistic doesn't mean you ignore the obstacle or deny the reality of the hardship. It means you look for the silver lining and recognize that the situation is temporary. It enables you to say, "Yes, we have a problem here, but I am committed to X and here's what I need to do to get there." Optimism multiplies the effectiveness of your commitment and persistence, making it even more likely that you will reach your goal.

WHAT RESILIENT LEADERS DO

As mentioned, we all have the capacity to develop and exhibit resilience, no matter what the challenge or change. This book is for leaders, however, so let's look at how the ability to adapt and thrive shows up in various leadership actions and mindsets.

LEARN AND ADJUST

Quickly learning and adapting to an increasingly complex work environment is one of the skills organizations seek out most. The most successful individuals, in the long run, are not the ones who know the most, but the ones who learn the fastest. Therefore, learning how to learn is key. It involves experimenting, reflecting, and figuring out how to improve next time. Resilient leaders are open to being wrong.

In the book *Why CEOs Fail*, David Dotlich and Peter Cairo discuss the concept of "self-blinding brilliance." Leaders who suffer from this condition see their way as the only way, and they are blind to any other possibilities. Because they've worked a certain way for years and for the most part their method has worked, they are inflexible and see no need to change. Such leaders are often perceived as defensive, aggressive, and dismissive bullies who feel the need to defend their position, rather than offer an option.

What happens when these leaders are faced with a different role, a company-wide restructuring, or new performance metrics where the old ways really don't work? They often run into an unyielding wall, trying the same things over and over while expecting different results.

In their willingness to experiment, reflect, seek feedback, and learn, resilient leaders are also resourceful. They don't feel the need to reinvent the wheel when solving a crisis. They are willing to learn from and build on the knowledge of others, adapting as necessary. Resilient leaders don't waste time on trial and error when they could be emulating a solution that's right in front of them.

FORM ROBUST ALLIANCES

As humans, our first instinct is and always has been self-preservation. As we evolved, we needed to defend ourselves against animals and people who wanted to do us harm. We adapted by forming mutually beneficial alliances both within and beyond our own species. One of our first alliances, for example, was with dogs: we took care of them and they protected us and helped us hunt. It was a symbiotic relationship.

We still need mutually beneficial alliances in the business world today. To advance in our fields and attain our goals, we must form networks and build relationships, which requires interpersonal skills. Defensiveness is innate; it was nature's gift to enable us to survive and persevere. The problem is that we sometimes apply defensiveness in the wrong situations—for example, when explaining the reason for our decision or answering an email request for a timeline update. We can unintentionally go into survival mode and, as a result, come across as distrustful or aggressive. This will not help us form mutually beneficial alliances. As you'll learn in Chapter 6, building relationships involves engaging people with openness and trust.

ACT WITH INTENTIONALITY

Adaptability by itself does not necessarily result in learning and resilience. Intentionality is a key component. Resilient leaders evaluate the situation, figure out what they need to do to adapt, and then execute a plan to get there.

My client Lewis epitomizes this intentionality quality. He came to me via the HR department because he had recently entered a high-level sales leadership role, and several people in the company had expressed concerns about his ability to do the work. Though Lewis had been with this multibillion-dollar organization for many years and had previously held high-level positions—he had managed the entire finance department before becoming the top executive in the marketing department—he had never been in sales. The stakes were much higher in this role since the company depends on his team's sales revenue. In addition, Lewis is somewhat of an introvert, which some felt was a bad fit in a role generally filled by more extroverted, cheerleader types. The naysayers' noise about Lewis's ability reached the board of directors and the CEO, who had appointed Lewis to the position but was now questioning his decision.

When I engage a new client, I usually use a 360-assessment to interview a range of coworkers who routinely interact with the individual and are familiar with their leadership style, skills, and behaviors. The feedback provides insight not only into how my client is perceived but also how others are impacted. When I interviewed people about Lewis, two attitudes became evident: skepticism and respect. No one questioned Lewis's integrity or talent, but they doubted whether he could handle his role—simply because he had never been in sales.

When I gave Lewis this feedback, he wasn't surprised. "When people get to know me, they realize I can do the work. But right now, this is a completely different organization with different people. I know what I need to do. I just don't know how to get it done faster."

Lewis needed to accelerate the process of gaining the trust of those at his new role. He needed to fill the relationship gap—that is, form robust alliances—with the influencers. During the process of the interviews, I identified a small set of individuals who were the most vocal, the most skeptical, and also happened to be the most influential in Lewis's sphere of operation—the ones making noise with the CEO and the board. We made a stakeholder list of six or seven people he needed to win over. Then we identified the level of support each person would provide him and the level of influence each person had in the company, and we mapped out steps to take to close the relationship gap with those who were making the noise.

The fact that Lewis had risen to the top in various roles and companies shows his adaptive capacity, but what made the difference here was his intentionality. He couldn't change the fact that many people doubted him, but he could take calculated steps to win them over, gain their support, build trust, and move forward faster. Lewis took the time to understand their concerns, needs, and wants and was intentional about finding the right strategy to adapt. When I later touched base with stakeholders who had been skeptical, their view of Lewis had radically changed for the better.

Lewis's intention was to build trust; yours might be to gain confidence or influence without authority. Whatever the case, resilient leaders learn to identify what they want to accomplish and let that intention drive their actions.

THINK OPTIMISTICALLY

When faced with crises, it is natural to become overwhelmed and even discouraged. However, resilient leaders don't stay in that mindset for long. They are able to see the situation for what it is and envision a different future. Their optimism allows them to prioritize and plan (commitment) and then take the necessary actions (persistence), no matter how difficult or challenging they might be, to make adapting and thriving a reality.

To remain optimistic, you sometimes have to ignore the naysayers, especially if one of them is yourself. During one Ironman race, I had to do just that. I was injured at the time and I wasn't in my best shape. My naysayer side thought, "You aren't ready. You didn't train hard enough. You will bunk." The optimistic me thought, "The race is long enough that if I feel sick, I can always take a break and continue, but I will finish." I listened to optimism and finished the race.

My client Ted was the CEO of a company he founded while in graduate school. As with most startups, Ted wore every hat in the beginning. As the company grew, he brought on people to share the load, but he didn't adapt to the changes and still wanted to be involved in every single decision. After he ran out of friends to hire, he finally started hiring senior people with more experience. The problem was that he treated these individuals like they were his college roommates, and that didn't go over well with more experienced, sometimes much older, employees. After interviewing some of these people, I learned that while they respected Ted as the founder of the company, they found him to be a strong micromanager, inexperienced, and naïve.

When I delivered this feedback to Ted, he was devastated, but he also took it as a call to action. He told me, "I want to be the best manager for these people. I want to be the leader everyone wants to have."

That vision and optimism turned into a commitment to an aspirational goal, which enabled him to take action in the present and start showing up differently at work. For example, he started asking for feedback and suggestions about how he could support his direct reports. He also started to see that there is more than one way of accomplishing a task, without compromising the outcome. As a result, he started passing the responsibility to his direct reports, which in turn reduced the amount of pressure and stress felt. Though it wasn't easy, this CEO had changed his management style 180 degrees within six months.

In making his commitment a priority, Ted also served as a role model. He didn't simply give lip service to change; he did it. The unintended consequence is that his attitude and behavior were an inspiration for other leaders in the organization.

Here are a few more characteristics associated with optimistic leaders:

- They are solution-focused and future-oriented thinkers.
- They are usually less afraid to take risks because they know that failing is part of being human.
- They are innovators.
- They display an attitude that tends to be contagious.
- They are usually more engaged at work and are better collaborators.
- They are found to be more ethical and have a better fit in organizational cultures.
- They are more adaptable and open to new ideas, which can help them find creative solutions to challenges and be more successful in the long run.

One recent paper concluded that there is a strong correlation between optimism and resilience.[4] In fact, optimism is

---

[4] Aruna Maheshwari and Varda Jutta, "Study of Relationship between Optimism and Resilience in the Times of COVID-19 among University Students," *International Journal of Indian Psychology* 8, no. 3 (July–September 2020).

an essential component of resilience, the multiplier of commitment and persistence. With zero optimism, you have zero resilience. Optimistic leaders tend to demonstrate behaviors and attitudes that support other leadership competencies and are usually part of a great leader's toolbox.

Overall, optimistic leaders tend to be more effective because they are able to create a positive work environment, inspire and motivate their team, and stay resilient in the face of setbacks.

LOOK IN THE MIRROR

Perhaps the best way to increase leadership effectiveness is to increase emotional intelligence (EQ), and the first step in that direction is to become more aware—of yourself first, and then others.

My coaching client Daniel was successful, driven, and hungry to move up the ladder. He had been identified as a high potential and was being groomed to get promoted. However, he wasn't moving up. In fact, he had been on that "high potential" list longer than others who had already been promoted.

After interviewing Daniel, his manager, and his direct reports and team members, I could see that his issue wasn't technical; he was meeting and exceeding his numbers every quarter. The problem was that Daniel was oblivious to the needs and wants of others, including his direct reports. His team wasn't happy, and many people had quit, transferred, or wanted out. Daniel didn't see this personnel turnover as his problem, since he was consistently performing well.

While important, technical knowledge is not enough to thrive as a leader. Being known as brilliant is great, but being a "brilliant jerk" is not. You need the people skills to collaborate and motivate. You need to be able to handle your own emotions under pressure, to show empathy toward others, and to be aware of the impact your leadership style can have. In other words, you need to develop EQ skills alongside technical skills.

According to *Fast Company*, EQ is the real secret to getting promoted faster[5]—which explained why promotion wasn't happening for Daniel. He seemed to lack empathy and an awareness of how his behavior affected his team. He needed to look in the mirror, become aware of his own style, and increase his EQ.

Unfortunately, I have met many individuals like Daniel, who lack awareness and as a result are reactive rather than proactive, taking actions based on habits that might or might not be appropriate for the specific situation. Such reactiveness comes from a lack of awareness on several levels:

1. *Awareness of self*: What are my needs, wants, desires, strengths, weaknesses, aspirations, and so on? What triggers me? What upsets me? The more you know about yourself, the better you are at adapting.
2. *Awareness of social context*: What are the wants and needs of those with whom I work? How do people act in this organization? What are the customs? What are the written and unwritten rules? The more you understand about the environment and the wants and needs of those working in that environment, the better you'll be able to adapt and respond to those wants and needs and eventually gain trust.
3. *Awareness of perceptions*: If you ask your stakeholders what

---

[5] Harvey Deutschendorf, "Emotional Intelligence Is the Real Secret to Getting Promoted Faster," *Fast Company*, May 24, 2017, https://www.fastcompany.com/40423640/emotional-intelligence-is-the-real-secret-to-getting-promoted-faster.

they think of you and they respond honestly, will you like what they say? Unfortunately, the higher you go in an organization, the less likely people are to provide candid feedback. Resilient leaders are relentless about asking for feedback. They want to know how others perceive them and how their actions impact others.

When we lack awareness of how we show up and the impact we have on others, we can develop blind spots. In his book *Leadership Blindspots*, Robert Bruce Shaw says these unrecognized weaknesses can hinder our success. Becoming a better leader requires courage, in particular the courage to find out how others see us. Leaders are in the business of moving people, and by understanding how others perceive them, they are more likely to connect with others, form stronger connections, gain influence, and ultimately move people to action.

The reality is, you cannot fix a problem if you don't know it exists. Blind spots are like that piece of food that you have stuck on your chin: you cannot see it unless you look in the mirror or unless someone has the courage to tell you that it is there. Resilient leaders invest their time in building social resilience, a community of trusted advisors who have the courage and the empathy to point out the piece of food stuck on the leader's chin.

PURSUE A LIFE PURPOSE

Why do we do the things that we do? Why do leaders seek promotions? Why do they try to grow leadership skills or gain more influence? It's easy to get caught up in our never-ending task list, in the expectations that we place on ourselves or that we think others have for us, and we miss out on opportunities to prioritize and, more importantly, to become resilient by living a life purpose.

In his book *Start with Why*, Simon Sinek says if we start with why—our purpose or mission in life—it makes everyday tasks and decisions much easier. It allows us to find fulfillment in the most mundane chores.

I hired a *why* consultant, Lee Prosenjak, to help me figure out why I do the things I do. That self-review helped me to see that my why is *to reframe the moments that matter so that we can adapt and thrive*. Knowing that statement has considerably changed the way I see things, the way I coach, and how I approach day-to-day activities. It has allowed me to stay committed to the task of writing this book, despite the challenges involved in doing so.

My second wife, Rujeko (you'll read more about this wonderful human later), is a medical doctor who works long, exhausting hours filled with overwhelming pressure at times, yet she remains compassionate and dedicated to her job. One day I asked her, "How do you keep doing this day after day?"

"It is brutal," she replied, "but I am grateful that my job has a lot of meaning to me. I want to help people get healthier."

Research has shown that having a purpose predicts better emotional recovery following a negative experience, even a negative experience like working long hours under tremendous pressure. People who have a clear idea of what they're striving for and why are much more likely to stay strong when things get tough. In other words, they are more likely to stay committed to their goal and persist in achieving it, with the end result being higher levels of resilience.[6]

---

[6] Stacey M. Schaefer et al., "Purpose in Life Predicts Better Emotional Recovery from Negative Stimuli," *PLoS ONE* 8, no. 11 (2013), https://journals.plos.org/plosone/article?id=10.1371/journal.pone.0080329.

WHAT RESILIENT LEADERS DON'T DO

Based on the preceding qualities, you might have a picture of what a resilient person looks like. But how does a lack of resilience show up in day-to-day life? The following describes a few behaviors that characterize people who haven't tapped into their innate adaptive capacity.

FEEL SORRY FOR THEMSELVES

We all experience highs and lows. It's okay to be sad, frustrated, and angry at a missed opportunity or traumatic event. But we can easily slip into victim mode and remain stuck in that mindset.

With a victim mentality, we tend to view our problems as being bigger than everyone else's. We also tend to put a lot of emphasis on luck. If something bad happens, we think ourselves unlucky and wonder, *Why do bad things always happen to me? What do I always find myself in this situation?* I have fallen into this thinking when someone else wins the lottery (*Why not me?*) and when I was first diagnosed with a brain tumor (*Why me?*).

The reality is that we all face hardship and adversity. We are not responsible for the things that happen to us, but we *are* responsible for how we respond.

When we feel sorry for ourselves in this way, we tend to complain. A lot. When we get stuck in seeing the negative, we can't see the other side of the coin: the opportunities that changes and challenges present to us.

FOCUS ON THINGS THEY CAN'T CONTROL

Just like gravity, there are problems that are not ours to solve. Whether it's a tumor, car accident, job loss, or micromanaging boss, some things are outside of our control. People who lack resilience tend to focus on these gravity problems rather than problems they can solve, and as a result they remain stuck in anxiety, depression, and frustration. They also find it hard to see the steps they can take to adapt and thrive in the less-than-optimal situation.

After my client Stephanie was promoted, she struggled in her new position. Her main problem was the excessive workload, which she was trying to tackle on her own. I was brought in to help her manage her time and priorities.

When Stephanie took maternity leave, the company put someone in her role, but this person quickly found out he couldn't do that job alone and asked his manager for more resources, which he received—including a couple of new hires. Stephanie was livid, not because her replacement got help, but because she realized that it was in her control to ask for the same resources. She had been trying to solve her workload problem all on her own, when it really wasn't hers alone to solve. Instead of asking for help, she started assigning blame, mostly to herself for not being good enough to handle the workload. All along, she had simply needed to ask for help.

Some people bring suffering on themselves because they focus on problems they can't solve—at least not alone.

REPEAT THE SAME MISTAKES

Everyone makes mistakes; to err is human, surely. But why do so many people make the same error over and over again? The goal is to learn from those mistakes and avoid repeating them, but people who lack resilience don't. They make the same mistakes over and over while expecting different results, which is what Albert Einstein claimed to be the definition of insanity.

How many times have you made the same New Year's resolution—start going to the gym, pick up this hobby, get that promotion? Yet if we don't change our behavior, we keep missing the mark. It's a vicious cycle. We make the resolution, don't change our behavior, don't achieve the resolution, then get upset and start blaming ourselves. Then our confidence goes down and we start lowering our goals until eventually we decide it's time to simply give up.

What's missing here is persistence. If we can stick with resolution long enough by taking specific actions, we will see progress, which will give us momentum to keep going to the gym or engaging in that hobby.

Resilient people know how to experiment, reflect, learn from their mistakes, and commit to do better next time. The goal isn't to be perfect, but to continually improve, and that requires persistence.

EXPECT IMMEDIATE RESULTS

In general, we don't like to wait. We want immediate results. If we are diagnosed with high cholesterol, we take statins to lower it now. When we order something online, we want it in two days (thanks, Amazon Prime!).

Resilience is a process. It's an endurance race that involves deliberate practice, intentional action, and persistence. If we try something new and expect immediate results, we can become frustrated and demotivated when those results don't materialize. The truth is that progress isn't always obvious. We don't always get the instant gratification of visible measurable success or someone saying, "You're doing great!"

In 1972 Stanford professor Walter Mischel ran an experiment inspired by his five-year-old daughter and her friends. In this study, a child was given a choice: receive one marshmallow now or wait fifteen minutes and receive two. Years later, in a follow-up to that experiment, the professor found that the children who waited to receive two marshmallows were doing better in nearly every area of life: they received higher grades, scored higher on the SAT, enjoyed stronger relationships, and had lower body mass index.[7] Learning to wait seemed to produce better outcomes.

To help my six-year-old daughter build resilience, I've been trying a similar experiment. Alexis loves chocolate, so I'll offer her one square and tell her that she can eat it now or wait until after swimming and have two. At first, she cried, "Why are you doing this to me?" It was a real struggle. But now she waits. I recently asked Alexis what she learned from the chocolate experiment and she said, "If I wait, I can get double." That's exactly what I want her to learn: sometimes waiting brings bigger rewards.

YOU HAVE THE POWER

A few years ago when I started my coaching practice, I wasn't getting any traction, and I started to get anxious. I needed validation, I needed to feel productive, I needed to make money. So I decided to find a regular job where I could find these things.

Thankfully, a little voice inside my head spoke up and said, *Think of the possibilities in this business. Nobody told you it would be easy. Anything worthwhile requires a level of sacrifice, a level of effort and persistence.* In that moment, I decided to

---

[7] Walter Mischel, Yuichi Shoda, and Monica L. Rodriguez, "Delay of Gratification in Children," *Science* 244, no. 4907 (1989): 933–38, https://www.science.org/doi/abs/10.1126/science.2658056.

keep working my business and wait for the rewards a little longer.

Today, I am glad I didn't let go of my dream. Like the kids who waited for two marshmallows and experienced better life outcomes, I have experienced rewards that go beyond money: satisfaction, fulfillment, happiness, balance, and more.

The biggest gift that life has given us is the power of choice. The second is our adaptive capacity. The problem is that we often forget to use this capacity in our modern-day struggles, or we don't know how. Building resilience does take time, but it's something you can start right now, with small daily decisions to commit, persist, and hope. Making those choices consistently and intentionally will make you a better leader and human.

No matter what life throws at you, adapting and thriving starts by understanding that you have a choice, accepting the difficult situation as it is, and committing to take action. Only then can you see possibilities for moving forward.

RECAP: THE RESILIENT YOU

Resilience is not a special skill that only some people are born with. You already have what you need to adapt and thrive as a leader.

The Essence of Resilience

Resilience is the natural ability we all have to reframe situations. When we see things differently, we think differently, and when we think differently, we act differently.

What current challenging situation can you reframe?

What Resilient Leaders Do

Among other things, resilient leaders are optimistic. They don't spend time thinking of what could go wrong, but rather of the future possibilities.

Which of the "resilient leader" traits do you see in yourself? Which one do you want to grow in?

What Resilient Leaders Don't Do

Resilient leaders don't feel sorry for themselves or assign blame. They adapt and thrive.

Which of the "don't do" traits do you see in yourself? What one step can you take to change that behavior?

Chapter 2

AMOR FATI

"Amor fati—Love your fate, which is in fact your life."
—FRIEDRICH NIETZSCHE

- Loving your fate—your life
- Self-compassion—the art of giving yourself permission not to be perfect
- Carrot, egg, or coffee—how do you respond to hardship?

After Sara and I learned I had a brain tumor, we met with several neurosurgeons, and then I decided to have Dr. Chandler from the University of Michigan remove my brain tumor. During surgery, the doctor discovered that the reason I was experiencing hearing loss and headaches is that the tumor was partially blocking the drainage of spinal fluid, which caused my brain to swell. When they removed the tumor, the swelling became even more pronounced. The surgery created scar tissue, creating further blockage. Three days after the original surgery, Dr. Chandler went back in to install a cranial shunt. When the pressure of my brain reaches a certain level, a small pump activates and sends the excess fluid from the brain to my stomach through a long tube. I call it my brain toilet.

After almost a month in the hospital, I went home and started the long road to recovery, which included regular visits with my doctor. During one such appointment, Dr. Chandler said, "I have good news and bad news, Luis. The good news is that the tumor was benign. Your recovery is going as scheduled, you're going to gain your health back, and you're not going to die. The bad news is that I was only able to remove about 40 percent of the tumor. The location made it impossible to remove more without doing real damage to the surrounding tissue. We'll have to monitor it over time."

"Okay," I said. "But I still get so tired and dizzy, and the double vision hasn't gone away. The worst part is how I keep forgetting things like my PINs, my Social Security number, and my phone number. I can't even add numbers in my head."

"I understand, Luis. And I think you have to accept your new reality. Cognitive dysfunction like you're experiencing is a frequent complication in long-term survivors of brain tumors and can be related to both the tumor itself and surgery. The good news is that these issues are usually not permanent. Your brain will likely adjust, but there's no way to tell how long it will take to return to full capacity. The reality is that you probably won't be able to do your job as a professor or walk straight for quite some time."

For months I had been stuck in my house, unable to drive, unable to read or focus or complete very basic cognitive tasks. I kept thinking all of these symptoms would go away and that I could return to teaching. I had put all my eggs in the basket of my career. Now I was faced with harsh identity questions:

Will I be whole again? Will I be able to return to work and pick up where I left off professionally?

A big part of my self-worth was wrapped up in my intelligence and academic accomplishments. People saw me as a "smart cookie." I had come to the United States on an academic scholarship, enrolled in university courses, and *then* started learning English on the side. I later got my PhD in four years at an institution where the average is six. I was a visiting assistant professor who was going to publish papers and eventually get tenure. In an instant, that was all taken away.

Based on the doctor's words, I started telling myself a story. He had said I would likely not be able to return to work soon, but I took that to mean I wasn't going to be smart. I wasn't even going to be average. After that appointment, my self-confidence plummeted. If I couldn't be a professor, what could I do? Who would I be?

At first, my wife was very supportive. Over time, however, she expressed frustration that I wasn't trying hard enough to get better. "I married a go-getter," Sara told me one day, "but I don't see that person anymore."

She was right. I had always been a positive person, but the surgery's impact on my cognitive abilities hit me hard, and I became discouraged at my lack of progress.

In those first months following my surgery, I became angry, frustrated, and ashamed, and as a result, I couldn't see the possibilities. People kept making suggestions about what I could do to improve, but I took that advice as condescending. They didn't know what I was going through. They didn't understand my reality. Their intentions were good, but I wasn't paying attention because I was so worried about people seeing that I wasn't as smart as I used to be.

It took a few months, but I finally came to accept myself

as I was, tumor included, and to realize that pre-tumor Luis no longer existed. I learned to embrace self-compassion and focus on progress, not perfection. This chapter provides key concepts to help you do the same, no matter what tough new reality you're dealing with.

LOVING YOUR FATE

Amor fati is a Latin phrase translated as "love of fate" or "love of one's fate." Ancient stoics used the term to describe an attitude in which someone sees everything that happens in life—including the bad things like suffering and loss—as good, or at least necessary.

Amor fati is the radical acceptance of the situation before you. It is not being in denial or slipping into a victim mentality, nor is it resigning yourself to just deal with it. *Amor fati* means loving your new reality and looking for ways to become a better person because of it.

"Frightened of change? But what can exist without it? What's closer to nature's heart? Can you take a hot bath and leave the firewood as it was? Eat food without transforming it? Can any vital process take place without something being changed? Can't you see? It's just the same with you—and just as vital to nature."
—MARCUS AURELIUS

This concept is clearly described by Ryan Holiday in his book *The Obstacle Is the Way*. Holiday proposes that we should get into the habit of embracing every situation and reframing each one to view it in a positive way. Even though certain events and circumstances are quite bad, we can always catch a glimpse of the silver lining. We just have to look for it.

How can you practically learn to love your fate? I see it as three steps:

1. Reframe
2. See the possibilities
3. Take action

We will repeat these three ideas in various ways throughout the book. The key to building resilience with *amor fati* is in seeing things differently, so you can think differently, so you can act differently. If you practice reframing, seeing the possibilities, and taking action now when you're not in the middle of a crisis, you will be ready when you are.

1. REFRAME

When Thomas Edison was about sixty-seven, a fire broke out at his lab. Someone rushed to his house to share the news, but by the time Edison and his son arrived, the fire was already out of control. In response, Edison told his son, "Go tell your mother and her friends, because they will never see a fire like this again."[8]

In the face of a real tragedy, Edison didn't wallow in what he lost. At some level he realized the fire was a gravity problem he couldn't solve at that moment. Instead, he *reframed* the negative situation in a positive light: an opportunity to view a spectacular fire, as well as a chance to get rid of rubbish and make room for more experiments.

---

8   Richard Feloni, "Thomas Edison's Reaction to His Factory Burning Down Shows Why He Was So Successful," Business Insider India, May 9, 2014, https://www.businessinsider.in/Thomas-Edisons-Reaction-To-His-Factory-Burning-Down-Shows-Why-He-Was-So-Successful/articleshow/34893119.cms.

Life is long enough that, sooner or later, you too will find yourself looking at a "fire" that's burning something valuable. How will you respond? The resilient response is to reframe—to look for the positives, however small.

To practice finding the positive, look for ways to reframe everyday situations you view as negative. For example, let's say you are stuck in traffic. Rather than getting upset and irritated, ask yourself, "What silver lining can I find?" You could listen to a podcast and learn something new, or get on the phone and call a friend you haven't talked to in a while, or contact that vendor you've been meaning to call. Learning to reframe in these less traumatic situations will prepare you to reframe when it really matters.

2. SEE THE POSSIBILITIES

Over the years, I have worked with several clients in Silicon Valley. During a meeting with one such individual—let's call him Daniel—I was supposed to share feedback I received during my interviews with his direct reports and peers. That feedback was not positive. People told me Daniel didn't listen and that he came across as disrespectful.

As soon as I started sharing some of his coworkers' perspectives, Daniel cut me off and started blaming someone else. In the first forty-five minutes of our conversation, I spoke very little.

Finally, I asked, "Can I share my experience with you?"

"Sure," he said.

"I feel unheard," I began, using the words coworkers had used in their feedback. "I feel disrespected. I feel you're not listening to me and that I cannot influence you. You're off-putting."

At that point, Daniel became really quiet. I thought, *Finally, I got his attention.* Boy, was I wrong. Encouraged by his silence, I continued to share, until he stood up and said, "You have disrespected me. This conversation is over." And he walked out. *What just happened?* I wondered.

A couple days later, HR called me. I was informed that Daniel had complained about his experience with me, and the company had decided to terminate my coaching contract. "We are here to protect our employees, and what you've done is unacceptable."

I was dumbfounded. "Can I tell you my side of the story?" I asked.

"No. We're not interested." And that was it. I had abruptly lost a contract that had provided 40 percent of my income. I wasn't even allowed to finish the engagements I currently had; they were transitioned to other coaches.

At first, I spun out in my mind. I felt like a failure, like I was a bad coach who had made a beginner mistake that cost me nearly half my income.

Then something stopped me. I realized I was viewing HR's feedback as the true reality. In actuality, their reality wasn't mine. I knew I had done my best to serve this client—not perfectly, perhaps, but I had treated Daniel with respect and had offered him true feedback from his direct reports. I asked myself one question: did I do my best at the time? The answer was yes.

Once I affirmed my reality, I asked myself another question: what am I going to do about this now? I was able to think about the possibilities. Then I asked myself, What did I learn from this situation? Could I have done something differently? How can I use this experience in the future?

Next, I used the Three Gifts Technique I often use with

my clients to reframe challenging experiences. This involves identifying three positive "gifts" or possibilities that could come out of the negative situation. In my case, not working with this company meant (1) I had more free time to go after higher-paying clients, (2) I had more time to work on myself, reflect on my work, and become a better coach, and (3) I wouldn't be dependent on one big company for a big chunk of my income.

Many leaders get stuck because they believe they don't have a choice. No matter how difficult your current situation is, there are always possibilities. When you pause to look for them, you put yourself in a place to move forward. And by the way, not doing anything is also a choice—perhaps not the right one, but still a choice.

3. TAKE ACTION

When you're dealt a "bad hand," what's your response? Do you fold? Or do you play it for all you've got?

If you're like the rest of humanity, you have probably said more than once "I'm so _____ [overwhelmed, stressed, tired, hopeless]." The question is, what do you do about it? When stressful things happened to me, I used to say things like "It is what it is" or "This too shall pass"—anything but deal with the crisis causing the overwhelm. It feels better to ignore it, or put it aside, or complain about it. The reality is that none of those responses improve the situation. The only way to make things better is to act.

After I reframed the loss of my big client and identified three possibilities, I took action. I vetted bigger clients, honed my coaching skills, and most importantly, increased my number of clients. Today if I lose one client, my total income will not be affected the way it was when that Silicon Valley giant let me go. Ultimately, I am in a much better place today because I lost that contract.

By reframing the crisis and seeing the possibilities, you give yourself a goal—a destination—which allows you to take action, one step at a time. You may not have control of the situation itself, but you can control your response to it. You can refuse to succumb to the highly infectious Victimitis Syndrome: "There's nothing I can do" and "It's all their fault." It is choice more than chance that determines our circumstances.

I have had many conversations in which my clients say things like, "*If* I had this resource, I would be able to deliver the goal." "*If* I had a different boss, I would be more engaged and enjoy my work." "*If* I had joined the company earlier, my exit package would have been a lot better." At one point in my own life I thought, "*If* I didn't have this tumor, my life would have been a lot better."

None of these statements are true. They are hypotheses that will never materialize, so they will not affect the outcome that already took place.

In my own life, for example, I am the person that I am today—a better person—not *in spite of* the brain tumor, the loss of my identity, and the destruction of my professional dreams and my marriage but *because of* those things. I didn't see it at the time, but now I understand that these hardships actually gave me an opportunity to reinvent myself.

The more we think about the ifs, the more we tend to stay stuck instead of taking action. And if you're stuck in hating your circumstances or blaming someone else for what's happened, you won't be able to see which direction to go, which means you won't be able to take action.

We all have the power of choice. Exercising that power to

love our fate is the key to reframing it, seeing the possibilities, and taking action. So, what are you going to do about it?

SELF-COMPASSION

Self-compassion is the catalyst that allows us to learn *amor fati*. It energizes us to reframe, see the possibilities, and take action.

When we experience a difficult situation—a setback at work, for example—we tend to become defensive and blame others or berate ourselves, neither of which is helpful. Blaming others or ourselves is the easiest action to take and it may alleviate how we feel about the failure, but it comes at the expense of learning. In addition, it might lead to a self-assessment of our own potential that undermines our personal development.

Self-compassion is the alternative to defensiveness and blame. It is characterized by three key behaviors:

- People who possess self-compassion are kind rather than judgmental in relation to their own failures and mistakes.
- They recognize that humans are imperfect and making mistakes is part of being human.
- They allow themselves to feel bad over the failure but do not let the negative emotions take over. They acknowledge the mistake, learn from it, and move on.

In short, self-compassion is simply giving yourself permission to not be perfect.

Perhaps the most important part of self-compassion is that you honor and accept your humanness. Things will not always turn out the way you want them to turn out. You will encounter frustrations, experience losses, make mistakes, and fall short of your own expectations. That is all part of being human, a shared reality for all of us. The more you open your heart to this reality, the more you will be able to feel compassion for yourself and for all of your fellow humans in this amazing journey we call life.

It's important to note that self-compassion is not self-pity. When you feel self-pity, you become immersed in your own problem and forget that others have similar problems, that you are not the only person on the planet who is suffering. Self-compassion, on the other hand, helps us to see the related experiences of self and others without feeling isolated and disconnected.[9]

PROGRESS, NOT PERFECTION

For a long time after my brain surgery, I compared my present self with my former, pre-tumor self. I saw so many things wrong with the new me that I developed feelings of shame. Yes, I had an excuse for my memory lapses and my inability to add numbers, and "I had brain surgery. What is your excuse?" became my mantra—a way to deflect blame and to justify a lesser version of myself. With the shame came a sense of inadequacy and unworthiness.

A tipping point in my brain surgery recovery process was when I accepted that the old me was gone and accepted my new self, tumor included. In this acceptance, I extended compassion to myself that allowed me to appreciate my progress instead of expecting perfection. I gave myself permission to not be perfect.

---

[9] For practice in self-compassion, see "Self-Compassion Guided Practices and Exercises" created by Dr. Kristin Neff at https://self-compassion.org/category/exercises/, (last accessed Oct. 31, 2023).

Self-compassion doesn't mean denying that the situation is hard. Instead, we freely embrace things as they are and give ourselves permission to suffer, to say "this sucks," and to fail on our way to progress. At the same time, we reframe the situation to look for the gifts and possibilities. Self-compassion gives us permission to not deal with the gravity problem or the obstacle, but to instead look at the possibilities.

SELF-CONFIDENCE AND SELF-COMPASSION

During my recovery, one of the things I really wanted to do was drive on my own. When I went to the doctor so he could sign off on me driving, he put me in a simulator to test my skills. I did fine "driving" along a straight road, but when I came to a right curve, I turned left every time. It was clear I couldn't drive yet. I walked out of the doctor's office feeling like a complete failure, like I would never be able to drive again.

I headed into the simulator expecting perfection because I had driven thousands of times before. When I couldn't perform as expected, my self-confidence went down the drain. I was ashamed that I couldn't do something that appeared so simple. I actually hid the results from others, even from my wife, because I was afraid of what they would think of me.

Self-compassion is the opposite. It aims for improvement, not perfection. If I could go back to that moment again, I would reframe my experience in the simulation as "I'm not ready to drive *yet*"—not that I had failed. I simply hadn't recovered enough to be able to drive. I was improving, but I wasn't there *yet*.

A few days after my trip to the simulator, I decided to teach myself to drive. Rather than aiming for perfection—that is, getting in the car and actually driving to a destination—I decided to start with something easily attainable. At first, I simply sat in the car, started the engine, and pretended to drive. Then I tried driving slowly around the block. Then I started going a little farther away from home, until finally I was driving as I had before. Each step was an improvement that made me feel good about myself and ultimately brought me to my goal.

One of my clients was told he had weak interpersonal skills. Because of his inability to collaborate, Victor was put on a performance improvement plan, part of which included executive coaching. If he didn't learn to work with his team, Victor was at risk of losing his job.

During our first meeting, I asked Victor to list the relationships he needed to improve. The two people at the top of his list were very influential in the company. They also happened to be the two individuals whose relationship with Victor wasn't the strongest. Starting with them would have been too risky. Instead, I asked him to identify the safest individuals—the low-hanging fruit with whom he could start.

Victor approached these people and asked what he could do to be a better collaborator. He came back with four or five actions, which we compressed into one observable behavior: be curious and ask questions. He started implementing this behavior with the whole team, not just the people who had made the suggestions. Almost immediately, Victor reported that relationships had improved, so he continued with the next individual and the next, until he got to the top two—the "risky" high-influence individuals, with whom he showed vulnerability and a willingness to connect by asking what they needed from him. When he got there, the feedback he received was that he was already making progress in being more collaborative. In other words, starting with the safest individuals and implementing the feedback he received from them resulted in a change of perception by everyone.

By being kind to himself and starting in the safest place possible, Victor was able to make measurable progress, rather than starting with the two most challenging individuals and feeling like it was an all-or-nothing, perfection-or-failure endeavor.

People with high self-esteem or self-confidence experience happiness and motivation when they perform as expected and receive constant reinforcement. When things are not working as planned and they are not "winning," however, self-esteem suffers. Whereas self-compassion is free of judgment, of ourselves or others, self-esteem is based on our evaluation of how we match up with others.

It's not that self-esteem or self-confidence is bad, but self-compassion allows us space to reframe challenges, see the possibilities, and take action without the pressure of doing so perfectly. Self-compassion offers a healthier and more sustainable way to feel good about the bad things that happen. Because people with self-compassion are always looking to adapt and improve, they are more resilient. They regularly look for the next step, and they measure progress rather than perfection.

Self-esteem or self-confidence can offer a level of emotional resilience and stability, but only when we're performing as expected. Self-esteem involves ego and there's a certain degree of defensiveness attached to it, whereas self-compassion starts from the assumption that we're not perfect, nobody is, but we're making progress.

One interesting finding from organizational 360s is that in general, the higher someone's opinion of themselves, the less others think of them. The reverse is also the case, especially as relates to leaders. The most effective leaders consistently rate themselves lower than others do, which shows a level of humility.[10] They know they don't know everything, but at the same time, they don't beat themselves up over that fact. They extend themselves a measure of self-compassion.

Leaders who rate themselves higher often feel like they know everything. This self-confidence can be counterproductive when they encounter situations that reveal they in fact don't know everything. In a sense, self-confident people are fragile because they are unable to bounce back, adapt, and change, whereas self-compassionate people are more likely to accept that they are wrong. They are more flexible.

A self-compassionate leader is also a better leader. Self-compassion is usually linked to compassion for others; as a result, these leaders extend the same nonjudgmental attitude toward team members that they show themselves. In addition, self-compassion triggers and encourages a learning mindset. With such an outlook, leaders are more likely to provide feedback that helps their direct reports grow and improve.

In the past, the most confident person was likely to climb the corporate ladder. Now self-confident people are the ones falling off the ladder because they can't adapt. The world is moving so quickly that it's impossible to be perfect all the time. Accepting that we might be wrong, not defending ourselves, and not insisting things go a certain way gives us freedom to sit back, learn from others, and ultimately become more resilient.

---

10   Jack Zenger and Joseph Folkman, "We Like Leaders Who Underrate Themselves," *Harvard Business Review*, November 10, 2015, https://hbr.org/2015/11/we-like-leaders-who-underrate-themselves.

CARROT, EGG, OR COFFEE: HOW DO YOU RESPOND TO HARDSHIP?

I've heard a story more than once about a young girl who went to her grandmother and told her about how hard life had been.

"I don't know how I'm going to make it," she told her grandmother. "I feel like giving up. Every time I solve one problem, another one arises."

The grandmother took the little girl to the kitchen and filled three pots with water. She placed each pot on one of the burners and turned the flame to high. Soon, the water in each came to a boil.

In the first pot, the grandmother placed some carrots, in the second she placed some eggs, and in the third she placed ground coffee beans. Without saying a word, she let all three sit and boil for about twenty minutes and then turned off the burners.

She fished out the carrots and placed them in a bowl. Then she took out the eggs and placed them in a second bowl. Finally, she ladled out coffee and placed it in a third bowl.

She turned to her granddaughter and asked, "What do you see?"

"Carrots, eggs, and coffee," the girl replied.

The grandmother brought her closer and asked her to feel the carrots.

"They're soft," the girl said.

Then the grandmother asked her to take an egg and break it. The girl cracked the shell and then peeled it off, revealing a hard-boiled egg.

"Go ahead and sip the coffee," the grandmother said. The girl smiled as she tasted the rich, flavorful drink.

"What does it mean, grandmother?" the girl asked.

"Each of these objects faced the same adversity, boiling

water, but they reacted differently," the grandmother said. "The carrot went in strong, hard, and unrelenting. However, after being subjected to the boiling water, it became softened and weak. The egg had been fragile. Its thin outer shell protected the liquid interior. But after sitting in the boiling water, its insides became hardened. The coffee grounds were unique, however. After they were in the boiling water, they changed the water."

The grandmother paused and looked at the girl. "Which are you?" she asked. "When adversity knocks on your door, how do you respond? Are you a carrot, an egg, or a coffee bean?"

We should all ask ourselves this same question: How do I respond to adversity? Am I the carrot that seems strong, but with pain and adversity wilts and becomes soft and loses its strength?

Am I the egg that starts with a malleable heart, but changes with the heat? Did I once have a fluid spirit, but after a death, a breakup, or a financial hardship, my outer shell looks the same, but on the inside am I bitter and tough with a stiff spirit, and a hardened heart?

Or am I like the coffee bean? The bean actually changes the hot water, the very circumstance that brings the pain. When the water gets hot, it releases the fragrance and flavor.

If you are like the coffee bean, when things are at their worst, do you get better and change the situation around you? When the hours are the darkest and trials are their greatest, do you elevate to another level?

Sometimes it feels unnatural to be grateful for things you didn't want to happen in the first place. But if you reframe the situation, see the possibilities, and take action, you can learn to love your fate and thrive in the midst of it. Like the coffee, you can transform your circumstances into something new and better.

Next, we'll introduce the resilience framework and consider the mental, physical, spiritual, and social components of resilience.

RECAP: *AMOR FATI*

Resilient leaders have an attitude whereby they not only accept everything that happens to them, including adversity and loss, but they actually love it and use it.

Loving Your Fate

When things are not going the way you want, don't get all bummed out and frustrated. Instead, take a moment, breathe, and ask yourself, "What am I going to do about this now?"

What is one current situation where you see the need to apply *amor fati*?

Self-Compassion

Give yourself permission not to be perfect. After all, making mistakes is part of being human.

Can you think of one area where you struggle with self-compassion?

Carrot, Egg, or Coffee

How do you handle the hard times? Are you the carrot, the egg, or the coffee?

Here's hoping you choose to be coffee.

Chapter 3

PILLARS OF RESILIENCE

"Enjoy the process of being a work in progress. It is a lifetime ride."

—ANONYMOUS

- The additive value of resilience
- How to approach the pillars
- Intentionality is the key

In 2012, I attended a conference where I met Jim Kouzes, author of *The Leadership Challenge*. During lunch, I happened to be fortunate to sit at his table. I shared the short version of my story of growing up poor in Guatemala, coming to the United States, being diagnosed with a brain tumor, and reinventing myself to adapt to my new reality.

When I was done, Jim said, "Luis, you need to write that down. It will make a great book."

"How am I going to do that? I'm not a writer."

"Just write your stories," Jim replied.

So I did. Three or four months later, I called Jim to tell him I had finished. He helped me categorize my stories, and in the process, five themes became evident. As I looked at the common threads, I realized they held the answer to how I had been able to adapt and thrive. Without having the words in place or even seeing the connection to resilience, I had been living these pillars—and so had my father many years earlier. In the midst of each hardship, we had adapted and thrived by:

1. embracing the suck,
2. facing our fears,
3. building relationships,
4. finding our inner strength, and
5. solving for fulfillment.

Sometime after identifying these themes, I stumbled across the concept of posttraumatic growth in the book *Option B* by Sheryl Sandberg and Adam Grant. As I read, I realized this kind of positive change that results from life's crises is exactly what had happened to my dad and to me after our respective situations.[11]

Then I began reading about resilience and what resilient people do and started connecting the dots to what my dad and I had done. I found evidence, both academic and anecdotal, to validate my personal experience and that of my father.

---

11 If you want to read a seminal paper on posttraumatic growth, check out "Post-Traumatic Growth: Conceptual Foundations and Empirical Evidence" by Richard G. Tedeschi and Lawrence G. Calhoun. Psychological Inquiry 15, no. 1 (2004): 1–18, https://www.jstor.org/stable/20447194.

By making connections to what I read and by working with clients around the themes I had identified, I realized there was something solid to these five pillars. I also realized these were the tools—the what—that people could use to build resilience in every area of their life. As such, they formed the final part of the resilience-building framework introduced in Chapter 1:

- *Why*: to adapt and thrive
- *How*: with commitment, persistence, and optimism
- *What*: using the five resilience pillars

Over the last few years, I have seen leaders encounter various challenges and use this framework to reframe their crisis, see the possibilities for a different outcome, and take action to make it happen. In short, I have seen them adapt and thrive even though the situation itself didn't change.

Is this framework the only path to resilience? Not at all. Are the concepts revolutionary? No, I am not claiming to have discovered hot water. You're probably doing some of these things already. The missing element for many people is engaging in these behaviors with the intention of building resilience. In this chapter we'll consider the additive value of resilience, suggestions for approaching the framework in Part II, and the importance of intentionality in bringing it all together.

THE ADDITIVE VALUE OF RESILIENCE

As defined in Chapter 1, resilience is the process of adapting in the face of adversity, tragedy, and significant sources of stress.[12] That adaptive capacity resides in four components of

---

12 APA online dictionary, s.v. "Resilience."

the human makeup: mental, physical, spiritual, and social. As you deliberately practice all of the pillars in this framework—Embrace the Suck, Face Your Fears, Build Relationships, Find Your Inner Strength, and Solve for Fulfillment—you build those facets of resilience across all components.

Picture a barrel made of four vertical wood slats. If all four slats are the same length, the barrel can be filled to capacity. However, if one piece is shorter than the others, then the barrel can only be filled to the height of the shortest piece. It doesn't matter how long the other slats are. Those slats represent the mental, physical, spiritual, and social components of resilience. If one is underdeveloped, resilience as a whole cannot develop to full capacity.

At the same time, there's an additive value to resilience. As you exercise each component, you strengthen your resilience as a whole.

In plant biology (remembering my days as a professor), *additive value* refers to the fact that the value of a trait expressed by a plant is controlled by multiple genes. If a plant is resistant to a certain disease, that resistance is the result of the expression of multiple genes acting together to strengthen that trait. Likewise, several genes are involved in a plant's ability to grow. The plant will grow in proportion to the degree to which those genes are expressed in their entire capacity. Each individual gene reduces or amplifies value to that genetic potential.

The same is true of resilience. The level of your overall resilience is impacted by the expression (or lack of expression) within each individual component. Lacking in one limits the expression and potential of the rest.

MENTAL RESILIENCE

Think of an athlete who is physically strong and able to withstand pain and suffering. Despite this high level of physical resilience, the athlete may lack mental resilience and thus never reach their full potential.

Mental resilience is the ability to mentally and emotionally cope with a crisis by motivating ourselves to do something difficult. It is also the unemotional component of decision making that allows us to learn how to learn, to understand where we are and where we want to go, to separate the gravity problem from the problem that is truly ours to solve, and to figure out the next step and take it, as uncomfortable as it may be. The stronger our mental resilience, the stronger our commitment to adapt and thrive no matter what the situation. We can intentionally build mental resilience by challenging our brain to analyze, synthesize, and learn in different ways. One way to do that is by reading—a lot. Read books on a variety of topics by a variety of authors. You can also learn a new language, learn to play a musical instrument, write blog posts, solve hard puzzles—the possibilities are endless.

Another idea is to use the Three Gifts Technique mentioned in Chapter 2 to build mental resilience as it forces you to think differently about the negative situation in front of you, seeing the positive possibilities that can come out of it. Another way to build mental resilience is to deliberately live outside your comfort zone so that you acclimate to do mentally and emotionally challenging things. One of my dear mentors, David Peterson, does something different every day, and I took that to heart. For example, today I actually parked my car on the opposite side of the street, and I intend to do that the rest of the week.

PHYSICAL RESILIENCE

Physical resilience refers to literal physical strength developed by movement, lifting weights, running, swimming, and other activities. The stress we place on our bodies increases our ability to withstand pain and endure uncomfortable situations. The benefits of physical exercise go far beyond the body. It improves mental capacity as well as spiritual stamina. Whereas mental resilience enables us to plan for the finish line, physical resilience enables us to endure the physical discomfort necessary to get there.

Another part of physical resilience is physiology, or how the body functions. As the saying goes, "You are what you eat." A healthy body is able to engage in not only more physical activity, but also reading, thinking, and other resilience-building activities. Building resilience in one area allows us to develop it in others as well, thus increasing our resilience as a whole.

My wife tells me all the time, "Please go run. You are a better husband when you are tired." I laugh, because I know she's right. I find inner peace when I exercise, but it also can be a way to intentionally increase happiness, as well as hope, connection, and courage, as Stanford University lecturer Kelly McGonigal explains in her book *The Joy of Movement*.

SPIRITUAL RESILIENCE

When people think of spiritual resilience, they sometimes tie it to religion, which is one aspect. But it also involves finding your why and living a life of purpose through your beliefs, principles, values, and morals. It is the ability to invoke positive emotions when you need them—emotions such as optimism, curiosity, or joy. Spiritual resilience fills what I call our love tank and enables us to endure hardship and give more to others.

Like mental and physical resilience, spiritual resilience can be intentionally built. For example, I developed a daily gratitude practice with my children as a way to work on spiritual resilience and fill up my love tank. After a trip to the Academy of Science Museum in San Francisco, we bought a colorful rock at the gift shop. On the way to school each day, I hand each of my children the Gratitude Rock and ask them to tell me three things they are grateful for. Then they hand the rock to me and I do the same. Nathan finishes up by saying "We are the grateful family."

One time, we were stuck in traffic and we were late for school. My daughter said, "I am grateful for the traffic because it allows me to spend more time with my dad and my brother." Alexis reframed something unpleasant and found something to be grateful for as a result of the situation, not despite the situation. That day, I was very happy for her.

This practice affirms that there is goodness in the world that benefits us daily. Looking for the silver lining in everything trains us to be grateful in situations that aren't too pleasant, which enables us to persist, grow, and thrive.

There are other ways to build spiritual resilience, for example, journaling, meditation, fasting, and volunteering. Each of these activities helps us build those positive emotions. In terms of resilience, training our spirit to be thankful and optimistic and joyful is just as important as training the mind or body.

One of the great things about spiritual resilience is that, unlike physical and even social resilience, it is not lost or impaired with physical disability because it does not depend on good health.[13]

---

[13] Lydia Manning et al., "Spiritual Resilience: Understanding the Protection and Promotion of Well-Being in the Later Life," *Journal of Religion, Spirituality and Aging* 31, no. 2 (2019): 168–86, https://doi.org/10.1080/15528030.2018.1532859.

SOCIAL RESILIENCE

Social resilience is the ability to reach out to others when you need help. It is more than fulfilling friendships; it is not equivalent to warm hugs and unconditional positive regard or a mutual sense of camaraderie instead of competition. It is about nurturing the right relationships with the right individuals.

To be able to reach out to these others in time of need, those relationships must be in place before the crisis occurs. Building those kinds of relationships means that we also need to be the kind of people others are likely to support, encourage, and trust. Like the other components of resilience, we need to take time to build those connections every day, maybe by mailing a "thinking of you" handwritten note or publicly recognizing the contributions of others, on LinkedIn for example.

It is easy to underestimate the importance of social resilience. We wouldn't blindly head into a business deal or hope resources will magically appear when we need them, yet we tend to approach relationships with that lack of planning. It is a myth that ideas stem from solitary genius or the lone inventor; rather, it is serendipitous conversations with people from different perspectives that fuel innovation. We can learn from the workshops of the renaissance, where artisans met and worked with architects, mathematicians, engineers, and biologists. The result was innovation that generated great social and economic value for all.[14]

Socially resilient individuals also value diversity and the different perspectives, values, backgrounds, and priorities it brings to the table. They don't merely accept diversity; they

---

[14] Piero Formica, "The Innovative Coworking Spaces of 15th-Century Italy," *Harvard Business Review*, April 27, 2016, https://hbr.org/2016/04/the-innovative-coworking-spaces-of-15th-century-italy.

intentionally incorporate diverse perspectives into group activities. Non-resilient individuals seek to eliminate diversity by excluding individuals who are different.

Having this kind of intentional relationship-building strategy allows you to be fulfilled day to day and have winning alliances when you need them most. This defense mechanism has an incredible level of complexity and symbiosis. As seen in the earlier example with Lewis in Chapter 1, the more you close the relationship gap, the more you benefit, and the more value you add to other people's lives.

To help my children build social resilience, I've started asking them a question at the end of each day: who did you help today? Knowing that I'm going to ask, my kids intentionally look for someone to help. This repetition helps them build a positive habit, as well as resilience.

HOW TO APPROACH THE PILLARS FRAMEWORK

If you approach the next five chapters looking for content, you're going to be disappointed. I'm not offering a magic key or be-all-end-all checklist. This is not a how-to book in the sense that you're going to gain step-by-step instructions for building relationships or embracing the suck. This is not "Resilience for Dummies," where I'm going to spell out the steps you need to take to end up a resilient person.

Instead, I'm offering concepts for you to consider and then apply in your own life. Read each chapter actively, making connections to your situation, identifying where you are not accepting reality as it is or what fears are going unchecked or what relationships you're lacking. Then make a plan to take the first step.

In case you're wondering about the order of the pillars, it

does matter to some extent. Embrace the Suck is first because you have to accept the situation as it is before you can work on the other concepts. Face Your Fears is second because it is closely linked to Embrace the Suck in that it covers the way you initially deal with the hardship or change. The final pillar, Solve for Fulfillment, ties the other four together. In a sense, learning the concepts in the final pillar makes it easier to deliberately practice the other four on a daily basis. No matter which pillar you're working on, remember the *how* aspect of the resilience framework: commitment, persistence, and optimism. These drivers will enable you to use these five pillars most effectively (Figure 3.1).

Figure 3.1

INTENTIONALITY IS THE KEY

Intentionality is living with a mindset of preparing for the future while also growing as a human being. As you deliberately build your resilience muscles, you also become a better person.

For example, most of us live by the law of random relationships: we happen to meet someone, we connect, and we develop a relationship. What I'm suggesting is that we go about building relationships, and the other pillars, with intentionality: thinking about who we want to connect with and how we're going to go about building those relationships with an eye toward forming robust alliances. The unintended outcome is that these alliances will be there, willing to help, when we most need them.

In a documentary about his life, Seymour Bernstein said that the real essence for what we are resides in our talent, whatever that talent is. For Bernstein, that talent was piano. He was a virtuoso who gave up a successful concert career to teach music. He wanted to be the best piano teacher, and he approached that goal with intentionality in every area of his life.[15]

Like developing talent, building resilience results from intentionality. If we're deliberate about building our resilience muscle, then every conversation, decision, and action will be an opportunity to exercise it. When we work on facing our fear (the second pillar), we can do so with the intent of building resilience. When we solve for fulfillment and strive to live out our purpose (the fifth pillar), we can do so with the intent of building resilience. The individual pillars will likely help you improve various areas of your life, but put them together

---

15 *Seymour: An Introduction*, 2014, https://www.imdb.com/title/tt2219650/.

under the umbrella of resilience, and you'll experience the true additive value.

TAKE THE FIRST STEP

Building resilience is a process. It begins with taking the first step right where you are, no matter what the challenge. As you'll see, you're not the only leader encountering stifling, frustrating situations with seemingly no solution. You'll also see that other leaders have learned to see things differently, think differently, and ultimately act differently in a way that creates unintentional positive outcomes, both for themselves and others.

Oftentimes we believe that a complex problem must have a complex solution, and that is not necessarily true. Even if the solution is complex, it is composed of a series of small, simple steps. When we think of the solution as complex, we often wait—or procrastinate—until we think all the pieces are in place. The truth is, we don't need to tackle the whole problem at once. We simply need to take the very first step, and we already have everything we need to do just that.

Are you ready to dive in?

RECAP: PILLARS OF RESILIENCE

To adapt and thrive, we need to build all facets of resilience—mental, physical, spiritual, and social—and we need to do so with intentionality.

The Additive Value of Resilience

The level of your overall resilience is impacted by the expression (or lack of expression) within each individual component: mental, physical, spiritual, and social.

Where are you currently strongest? Which one do you need to strengthen?

Intentionality Is the Key

Like developing talent, building resilience results from intentionality. If we're deliberate about building our resilience muscle, then every conversation, decision, and action will be an opportunity to exercise it and strengthen it.

What step can you take right now to strengthen your _____ [enter your answer from above] resilience?

Part II

THE PILLARS OF RESILIENCE

Chapter 4

EMBRACE THE SUCK

You can't control the rain, but you can choose whether or not you get wet.

- *Accept* things as they are.
- *Envision* the possibilities.
- *Execute* the steps to realize your goal.

After I finally recovered enough from my brain surgery to think about going back to work, I was faced head-on with the question that had been nagging me since the follow-up appointment with the doctor: what am I going to do now?

The professor I worked with at Michigan State University wanted me to come back, so I did. My coworkers and students were very supportive, but I struggled. I kept forgetting things and making mistakes doing basic things. Finally, I got so frustrated that I decided to go elsewhere rather than losing face.

Around the same time, Sara was offered a job in Houston, and she really wanted to move to a warm, sunny place. I decided I needed a reset, so I agreed to go.

I applied for jobs in Houston, including a couple of postdoctoral positions at Rice University and the University of Houston. My professor at Michigan State gave me incredible recommendations, and a professor at Rice University hired me right away.

A few months into my new position, however, it became clear that I couldn't perform as expected. The professor knew I had undergone brain surgery, but she didn't know the level of difficulty I was having with designing experiments and keeping track of the materials and results. It wasn't pretty. Shortly thereafter, I quit because I simply couldn't do the work. The truth is, it was likely only a matter of time until she let me go. We had discussed my lack of progress on a few occasions, and quitting was a last attempt to maintain some sense of control and save me the humiliation of being fired.

In addition, Sara and I were having more trouble at home, and less than a year after we relocated to Houston, she announced that she was moving to the Middle East for another job. She pointed out that she was the breadwinner, and that meant her career determined where we lived. She was right, but hearing her say it added another layer to the shame I already felt—not because she was doing better than me, but because I couldn't do my part. Still, we decided that she would go ahead, and I would wrap things up in Texas and then move.

A month or so after Sara left, one of her sisters needed information that I could only obtain by going through my wife's email. We shared passwords and did this kind of thing often, so accessing her email wasn't out of the ordinary. What I found, however, *was* out of the ordinary. Based on a series of emails, it became clear that Sara wasn't in love with me anymore, and her move to the Middle East was part of her strategy to end our marriage.

I sat at my dining room table and cried like a baby. I had no career, no direction, and apparently, no wife.

I moved from the table to the kitchen floor and curled up into a fetal position, agonizing over what my life had become. I didn't want to be a burden to my family, and I had no support system in Houston. Would I ever recover my mental capacity so I could become a professor? If not, what was I going to do? Who would hire me? I couldn't see a way out.

With that thought, I decided the only option was to end it all. I couldn't imagine going on without Sara. She was my sole support at the time, and I loved her with all my heart. I felt so devastated and helpless at losing her on both levels that I started thinking about how I would exit this world and escape my misery.

Then, out of nowhere, I thought of my mother.

How could I do that to her?

My mom would suffer tremendously if I took my own life, not only because she would lose a son but because she was a practicing Catholic and viewed suicide as a grave sin. She would see this act as a relinquishment of my place in heaven.

Thinking of my mom brought me back from that dark place. It prevented me from following through and gave me a moment to pause and think more rationally: *okay, what am I going to do about this?*

That question is the first step forward, a call to action.

This chapter provides a mental model for looking at life's challenges through a different lens, one that enables you to accept the situation, envision a different future, and execute the steps to get there. This chapter is where you start when you're not sure what to do next.

ACCEPT

When I was coping with the new reality of no longer being a professor, I was living under certain assumptions: *Something is wrong with me. I am not the same person I used to be. I am irreparably flawed.*

I felt I wasn't even a shadow of the person I used to be, and this left me with a deep sense of unworthiness and shame. I compared myself to people who started their careers when I did, some of whom were already working toward tenure. Even worse, I kept comparing myself to my former self, and that person was gone.

These comparisons left me feeling deficient, which is an invisible toxic gas that suffocates and inhibits. It was at the core of my inability to move forward. I felt trapped, unable to see the possibilities of what else I could become.

Outside feedback seemed to confirm my fears. The doctor told me I wouldn't be a professor, that I wouldn't be able to speak clearly or walk straight. My wife told me she had married a future professor, and now that wouldn't happen. I treated this feedback as truth, something I had to accept, and that added to my sense of unworthiness.

My feelings of deficiency went hand in hand with the feelings of separation from my wife. If I was defective, how could I possibly think about getting better and winning her back? How could I consider belonging in a wider sense?

It was a vicious cycle. The more deficient I felt, the more separated I felt from my wife, my colleagues, and my hopes and dreams.

The problem was that I was looking backward—at what I had before in my health, my marriage, and my social standing in the world—instead of realizing where I was at the moment.

RADICAL SELF-ACCEPTANCE

We need to take charge of our pain and struggle, our needs and wants and aspirations, *as we are*, in the midst of the hardship or new reality. Radical self-acceptance means we see the good, bad, and ugly about ourselves, without ignoring the parts we don't like. In my case, I needed to accept that I wasn't the same person I had been before. At some point, I realized that I could keep moping about the fact that I couldn't continue in the profession I trained for and loved, or I could accept the new me—Luis Velasquez, tumor included. I didn't have a choice about how I got there, but I did have a choice about moving forward. This kind of radical acceptance allowed me to say, "Okay, this is me. What can I do with what I have?"

It might not be your fault that you had a brain tumor, or that you grew up in poverty, or that you ended up in a toxic work culture, or that the pandemic eliminated your job, but it is your responsibility to figure out what to do next. Self-acceptance isn't an excuse to become complacent and accept the status quo. You have the power to choose what's next.

One aspect of radical self-acceptance is recognizing that we all have moments of self-doubt and insecurity. When I met Nikita, she was in a bad place emotionally. She had created stories in her head that she wasn't good enough, which caused her to fear that she would soon get fired for falling short.

"Where are these stories coming from?" I asked during one of our meetings.

"It's the feedback I'm getting," she replied.

"Who's giving you this feedback?"

"My boss. He knows me. He knows that I should be doing more."

Fast-forward a few months. The company reorganized, and as a result, Nikita's boss moved to a different department. As part of the reorganization process, Nikita met with the founder of the company, who said, "Nikita, you are incredible. We want you to stay where you are and run the project. You're moving it along quite well."

Suddenly, Nikita had new information. Based on her boss's feedback, she had created a story in her head that she wasn't good enough, that she wasn't adding value. Now she understood that wasn't the case. Radical self-acceptance involves understanding where you are while simultaneously challenging known perceptions by seeking other data. After Nikita heard the founder's "data," I encouraged her to seek out more. She soon discovered that other people also thought she was doing a great job. Nikita learned that the way she was seeing herself based on her boss's feedback alone wasn't the absolute truth, but a story that could be debunked.

WHAT AM I GOING TO DO ABOUT THIS?

In the face of hardships or crises, I used to say, "Well, it is what it is." That statement communicates an acceptance of things as they are, but it leaves off the next step of figuring out what we're going to do about it. If we're to grow in resilience, we need to make this mindset shift. It allows us to move beyond surviving and look for solutions.

With many of my clients, performance reviews and other feedback are a source of struggle that leaves them feeling discouraged and stuck. In the same way that we cannot control gravity problems, we cannot control feedback given. We can only control how we respond. Rather than being paralyzed by negative feedback, ask yourself if there is some truth to it. Then let the question "What am I going to do about it?" become your call to action, the affirmation that signals you are ready to move on.

PLAY TO YOUR STRENGTHS

After you've accepted the situation and given yourself space to ask what you're going to do, it's time to start moving forward.

According to the 360 interviews I conducted, my client Isaac was perceived as disengaged and aloof. He is a tech introvert who only speaks up when he has something meaningful to say, but in the context of meetings, his peers and superiors viewed this disposition negatively. One person commented that Isaac "needs to show up more. He needs to be engaged as if he cares or knows what is going on."

When I presented this feedback to Isaac, he took it hard, but he didn't get stuck. Together, we came up with a plan in which Isaac could use his strengths to change the negative perception.

According to the 360 data, those strengths included the leadership style he already had. Most of his direct reports said Isaac was one of the best managers they'd ever had. Other feedback was that these directs wanted to have more visibility with other parts of the organization. So, as part of his development strategy, Isaac started bringing his direct reports to some of his meetings and letting them answer questions and give reports, while he still remained silent unless he had something important to say. Follow-up interviews with the same stakeholders revealed that the behaviors previously viewed as disengaged and aloof were now seen as empowering to direct reports. They saw Isaac as someone who develops his people. Soon after, he received a promotion.

If Isaac had taken the original feedback as something he needed to accept and respond to, he might have started acting differently, even though speaking out for the sake of appearing engaged wasn't authentic for him. Instead, he played to his strengths: developing and empowering his direct reports. By making visible the actions he had already been taking with his people, Isaac changed key stakeholders' perception, which had the unintentional consequence of accelerating a promotion.

ENVISION

I was born in San Pedro Sacatepéquez, in the western region of Guatemala, and throughout my childhood, our country was a bastion of violence. Over the course of the civil war that lasted from 1960 to 1996, more than 200,000 people died.

My family was never directly involved in the fighting, but my father saw the effects as he traveled across the country in his job as a truck driver. Plus, we couldn't escape the war's effects since my father worked for his father, a merchant, who made his living off trade and commerce.

Perhaps without realizing it, my parents taught my siblings and me to have aspirations in the midst of these hardships. They never communicated a sense of "Oh, poor us. We're stuck in this horrible situation that will never change." Neither did they view us as a potential source of free labor and encourage us to leave school to become contributing members of the family—even though many parents in that region, including my grandfather, took this route. Instead, they taught us to think beyond the poverty and violence, and dream of something different. They would ask us questions like, "What do you want to be when you grow up? What kind of car do you want to drive? Where will you live?" In doing so, they planted a sense that we could reach for the stars.

Some research shows that the more struggles someone has early in life, the more resilient they become. However, you can't take advantage of opportunities to become resilient if you're not looking for them. People who are merely surviving have a hard time dreaming of more. They often live by an "it is what it is" attitude, which can cause them to be fatalistic and complacent, thinking things will never change. In terms of building resilience, having an aspirational goal is far more important than going through much suffering. Aspirations, hopes, and dreams—in short, optimism—are an incredible source of motivation if they are supported by the other drivers of commitment and persistence.

I first came to the United States on an academic scholarship. As I attended classes, learned English, and engaged in the culture, I realized how much I could achieve in this country. When I returned home at the end of my program, that vision motivated me to find a way back to the States so I could fulfill my dreams. My optimism fueled my commitment and persistence.

I now understand that this aspirational element has been key to my resilience. No matter how horrible the current situation, if you can dream, you can more readily move in a direction that may eventually move you out of the "suck." The presence of optimism does not necessarily signal an end to the distress, but rather the beginning to and the desire to move past it.

ASPIRATIONAL GOALS

The day after I was diagnosed with a tumor, Sara and I drove to Chicago for a wedding in which Sara was a bridesmaid. We had been planning this weekend away for months, and though we hadn't expected to receive such life-changing news that day, we couldn't do anything about it, so we decided to go ahead with our plans. It was a blessing to have the distraction of the wedding, but it was still hard. Both of us had that horrible news in the back of our minds the whole time, and no one else knew what we were dealing with.

The day after the wedding, my wife and I had planned to roam around the city before heading home. We ate breakfast and then I asked Sara if she wanted to go watch the Chicago Marathon, which happened to be taking place that day. I was curious about the event, but I was also looking for a distraction—something to take my attention away from the tumor growing inside my head.

Sara agreed, and we pushed our way to the finish line to cheer on the runners as they completed their race. As people passed us, we could see the emotion on their faces—the tears, the smiles, the pain, the sense of accomplishment. One person knelt after crossing the finish line and looked to the sky, presumably giving thanks. They weren't the fastest runners, but they sprinted to the end as if they were. They were completely running their own race, one probably far more significant than the marathon itself.

Then I noticed that many of these runners had signs on their shirts that read things like "Domestic Violence Survivor" and "Breast Cancer Survivor" and "Cancer Sucks." I was filled with admiration for these competitors, as well as inspiration. I could see myself crossing that finish line along with them, the words "Brain Tumor Survivor" written across my back.

I suddenly turned to my wife and said, "Sara, I want to run this marathon next year."

"Yeah, yeah," she replied.

"No, really, I want to run this marathon. Next year."

Sara looked at me with tears in her eyes. "What are you talking about? You have a tumor in your head. You don't know what's going to happen. You don't even know if you're going to be alive next year. What you're saying is crazy."

I shook my head. "No, no. I want to do this. And you're doing it with me!"

At this point she truly started crying. I kept pressing, and finally, I saw a little twinkle in her eye. "Okay, let's do it," she said with a small smile. We even shook hands on it.

Running the Chicago Marathon became my aspirational goal. It allowed me to envision the future I wanted: living and thriving beyond the brain tumor. It gave me a sense of control: I could make a training plan, run smaller races, and prepare my body and mind for the race. I was still uncertain about what the future would bring. I didn't know if I'd be alive next year or even next month. I was afraid for myself, for my wife, and for our marriage, unsure whether we'd be strong enough to get through this. But suddenly, despite all of my doubt, I had something to do next year. I was going to run a marathon.

An aspirational goal is something big, something that defies logic in different ways. When you set this kind of goal, you may not see a specific path to achieving it. You may be unsure when or if you will attain it. You simply know that this goal is very important to you and you will find a way to make it happen.

What is your marathon, your aspirational goal? What do you envision for your future—in spite of your current challenge? Do you want to become vice president of your company? Do you want to sell your business? I'm reminded of a popular saying often attributed to the artist Michelangelo: the greater danger isn't aiming too high and missing but aiming too low.

The *envision* aspect of embracing the suck involves asking yourself what you really want to achieve and how you will feel once you have it. For months after I committed to run the marathon, I repeatedly pictured myself crossing the finish line. I even practiced in front of the mirror, acting out what I would do the second I crossed the finish line in celebration of the accomplishment. As silly as that sounds, this routine gave me hope for the future (*optimism*), solidified my *commitment* to make it happen, and gave me power to *persist* through my doubts and grueling workouts. Remember the formula:

(commitment + persistence) × optimism = resilience

An aspirational goal acts as the accelerant, driving you to adapt and thrive. It sets the direction for your actions and gives you the inspiration to keep moving forward.

CHECK YOUR ASSUMPTIONS

To come up with an aspirational goal like running the Chicago Marathon or becoming CFO, you have to let yourself dream. To do that, you have to let go of the stories in your head and the assumptions you make about yourself, others, and your current situation. In the work world, the following questions, stories, doubts, and assumptions (and more!) often get in the way of envisioning what is possible:

- I am too old to change careers.
- I am too young to be taken seriously as a leader.
- I don't have enough education.
- I am overqualified for the role.
- I have too many challenges to overcome.
- I don't see a way to get support for my idea.
- My time has passed.
- "They" won't ever see me for that role.
- I don't fit the role, in terms of gender, race, religion, and so on.

While these statements might feel true, they are actually assumptions. And if you start believing these assumptions, they will stop you from dreaming, let alone taking the steps to reach your goal.

A few years ago, I went for a bike ride in the mountains and found it more difficult than usual. It felt like I was trying harder but not moving faster. Nevertheless, I kept riding.

When I finished the ride, I was tired and unhappy with my performance. As I loaded my bike into the car, I immediately noticed the problem: the brake pads had shifted and had been rubbing against my back wheel. I had ridden thirty-five miles with my brakes on. No wonder it was so difficult!

Have you ever driven your car with the emergency brake on? We all have. What do you do when you realize that it's on? You don't accelerate; you simply release the brake. The day of my frustrating bike ride, I didn't realize the brakes were on, so I just kept accelerating, trying harder and harder with no improvement. My frustration, and painfully slow progress, could have been avoided if I had simply checked the brakes ahead of time.

The brakes on my bike are like the assumptions we make about situations, ourselves, and others. These assumptions slow us down and impede forward progress. The answer is to release the brakes, to accept the way life is showing up, and then ask yourself, "What is possible now?"

I have seen this scenario play out over and over with myself and my clients. Assumptions get in the way of thinking about what is possible—what we could actually do if the brakes weren't there. Take Sandra, for instance. In our coaching sessions, Sandra and I had been working on elevating her executive presence. She had an opportunity to lead an important and visible project. She was confident in her ability to do the work and was sure it would lead to a promotion. Yet, at the last minute, Sandra told HR and her boss that she wasn't interested.

"Why did you do that?" I asked.

"I assume they will give the job to someone else anyway, a man or someone with much more experience," she said. "Plus, my boss doesn't think much of me. The reason I'm working with you is because he doesn't see me fit to lead."

I pointed out the flaws in her thinking: Sandra knew she could do the job, and she wanted the opportunity. In addition, she was working with me because her company saw her potential, not because she needed to be fixed.

"It's too late anyway," she replied. "I already told them I didn't want the opportunity."

"Saying 'it is too late' is another assumption," I said. Assumptions caused her to forgo the opportunity she wanted, and when I pointed out those assumptions, she responded with another assumption.

As it turned out, she wasn't too late. She walked into her boss's office and put her name in the hat for the project. She alerted her HR business partner that she wanted to move forward. In the end, she got the job.

Sandra's assumptions were the brakes she was unintentionally putting on her career, on her aspirational goal.

The next time you hit a challenge at work or feel pressured to perform, remember that you have a choice: you can look at the situation as a challenge or as an opportunity. The way you see it will determine how you react. If you see it as a challenge, the brakes will likely come on. If you see it as an opportunity, you can let go of the brakes and see what is possible. That's the power of having an aspirational goal.

WE CAN ALWAYS GET BETTER

When my parents used to ask those questions—"What kind of car are you going to drive?" "Where are you going to live?" "What kind of job are you going to have?"—they were giving my siblings and me aspirational goals in the midst of our gravity problem (poverty, war, etc.). As a kid, I didn't have the resources to buy a car, for example, but with this vision I could start moving in that direction. I could take the next step: get better grades, get into college, get a job, and so on.

One time I came home with poor grades. I had failed English. I showed my report card to my dad, whose only response was, "Oh, okay. That's good."

"That's the best I could do. I tried," I said, and my dad simply nodded.

A few days later, my grandfather had a load of wood delivered to our house. This wasn't new. Normally, he paid someone to chop the wood and then my family took as much as we needed.

This time, however, my dad handed me an ax and told me to start chopping. It usually took one man a few days to chop the truckload, so there was no way I could finish it on my own, but my dad wanted to make a point.

After about a half hour, I stopped and returned to our house.

"No, you need to finish it," my dad said.

"I can't do it," I replied.

"Yes, you can. That's what you'll be doing the rest of your life if you don't keep your grades up."

He never said, "You need to study. You need to get good grades." He gave me options and showed me what would happen if I made certain choices in relation to my schoolwork. I realize now that he was helping me to challenge my own assumptions, in this case, my assumption that I wasn't good at English. He showed me the potential outcome if I took that assumption as truth.

No one is perfect, but everyone has the ability to improve. If we view perfection as our top priority, we are living from a fixed mindset. From this frame of mind, we feel like we're being measured and judged and often falling short. We not only think we have to be right, if we're not we take that as proof that we can't do better. The assumptions we make about ourselves can and will increase the limitations we put in front of ourselves.

However, if we come at life from a growth mindset and put aside these assumptions, we can better focus on improving, on taking the first steps forward. When we reframe our situation and start seeing the possibilities, we will think differently and then act differently. We are the product of our actions, and our actions are the product of our mindset.

When my clients are in the midst of a challenge, I use the Three Gifts Technique to help them look for possibilities and opportunities. When they are not currently in crisis, I encourage them to use the Three Gifts in reverse as a way to envision and prepare for what might go wrong. When things are going well, for example, try asking yourself, "What could go wrong?" and list three possibilities. Then look at each one and consider what you could do now to prepare for that potential crisis.

Another exercise involves identifying three things you don't like about yourself in a certain situation and then taking steps to do the opposite. The Human System Dynamics Institute gives the following examples:

- Turn judgment into curiosity.
- Turn conflict into shared exploration.
- Turn defensiveness into self-reflection.

- Turn assumptions into questions.[16]

Considering the other side of the coin starts the process of improvement, reminding yourself that you can always get better.

When something bad happens, it's a call to action. When something good happens, it's a call to action. And guess what? The status quo is also a call to action. No matter what we're currently experiencing, it's an opportunity to improve, to increase our resilience. Always learning, always improving is the key to becoming even more resilient.

EXECUTE

The third "bucket" is all about taking action. After you accept yourself and the situation, after you envision what can happen, you have to act.

Taking that first step is often the hardest, though, isn't it? It requires us to take a risk and put ourselves out there. When clients tell me how hard it is, I usually ask one question: "What will happen if you don't do anything?"

After they pause and sometimes ask me to repeat the question, they'll say, "Well, nothing."

Exactly. If you don't execute after you accept the situation and envision how it could be different, nothing changes.

I guarantee you have what it takes to act. You just have to start moving.

---

16 Judy Oakden, "Standing in Inquiry—Why It Serves Us Well in Our Work and in Life," Human Systems Dynamics Institute, August 2018, https://www.hsdinstitute.org/resources/Standing_in_inquiry.html.

SOLVE FOR THE RIGHT PROBLEM

Before we can move forward, we have to make sure we're solving the right problem—a problem that is actually ours to solve. Sometimes we try to solve problems that are not really problems at all; they are *perceived* problems that result from negative rumination—obsessive negative thinking about the causes and consequences of a stressful event, situation, or choice, to the point where it interferes with normal mental functioning. These perceived issues can feel huge and overwhelming, but they usually can't be solved because they aren't real to begin with; we've created them in our minds.

Gravity problems, on the other hand, are real, but they are still not ours to solve. We have absolutely no control over gravity problems like a brain tumor or toxic boss, and we waste emotional energy if we obsess about solving them.

The only type of problem we can solve is a situational problem. It is something we can control and take steps to fix.

Once you separate the situational problems from the perceived and gravity problems, ask yourself three questions:

- Is this problem mine to solve?
- Is this problem mine to solve right now?
- Is this problem mine to solve with help?

From here, you can figure out the next steps to move forward.

The Tuesday after the MRI that revealed I had a brain tumor, Sara and I met with the neurosurgeon. As we waited, I was still holding onto a hope that the MRI had been wrong, that there was no tumor. In some ways, I hadn't really accepted my situation as it was.

When the doctor walked into the examination room, he

slipped two MRI films into the light display hanging on the wall, and then turned to us and asked, "Can you identify where the tumor is?"

I still remember the doctor's animated tone, like this was some sort of game. Plus, he was actually smiling.

I hesitated and then pointed to a small bright spot at the back of my brain.

The doctor shook his head and chuckled. "Nope," he said. "I always do this to test the patient's perception." Then he pointed to another spot on the film. "This is it."

A shock coursed through me. The spot the doctor pointed to was the size of a lemon. As the perceived severity of my situation sank in and I became more concerned, the doctor's smile turned into something more like excitement. He told me that I was the perfect candidate for a new approach he wanted to try and that he had asked the hospital to purchase some new equipment. It was as though he had won a prize at my expense and wanted to share his good fortune with us.

The tumor was my gravity problem. I couldn't do anything about the fact that it grew in my brain. However, I was in full control of what I was going to do about it, and I didn't want to be this doctor's guinea pig.

In the following days, Sara and I poured ourselves into finding the highest-ranked neurosurgeons in the nation. I stopped denying my condition and found out everything I could about the type of tumor, treatment options, and long-term outcomes. Even though some of the information was disheartening, doing this research gave me something to focus on and helped keep my fear at bay. It gave me a sense of purpose. Plus, I didn't know what else to do. I was a professor of biochemistry and research was my thing, so I challenged my assumptions and played to my strengths. In doing so, I could see a path forward.

I moved from a place of helplessness to one where I was taking control of my own destiny.

After visiting three neurosurgeons in three different states over the course of two weeks, I ultimately settled on a doctor at the University of Michigan. After talking with Dr. Chandler the first time, I realized that the purpose of our medical road trip hadn't been only about finding the most qualified doctor; it had also been about finding a doctor who knew my name and cared for my whole person.

I was still pretty scared about the idea of having brain surgery, and the more I learned about the challenges I'd be facing during recovery, the more uncertain I became about my future. But I also started to believe that I would get through this. It wasn't going to be easy, but I would be okay.

Could I control the fact that I had a tumor? No, that was my gravity problem. What could I control? My understanding of my situation, the person I chose to manage my care. Did I need to solve it immediately? No, I could take time to research, visit each doctor, and ask questions. Was it mine alone to solve? No, I needed Sara's help, plus the help of the doctor I eventually chose.

We can waste a lot of time and energy focusing on the gravity problem instead of the problems that are actually ours to solve. I once facilitated a leadership offsite, and we decided to have a working lunch. When the food arrived, Nate rifled through the bags and then announced, "There's no ketchup here. I can't believe they did this! I'm going to call and ask what happened." And then he got up and left the meeting.

Unfortunately, Nate was one of the key players in this meeting. We couldn't proceed without him.

All of a sudden, I understood why Nate was always overwhelmed and overworked: he poured his energy into solving the wrong problems, like finding ketchup, and didn't have enough time or brain space for the problems that were truly his to solve.

TRANSFORMATIONAL CHANGE, NOT A BAND-AID

As mentioned in Chapter 1, resilience is not a quick fix. Resilience comes as we experience deep, lasting transformational change, and this takes time. Though we yearn for change and experience its reality all the time—when thoughts become words, when our brains take sight and turn it into understanding, when we fall in love and become a different person—we still resist it. We all experience the constant struggle between accepting change and pushing it away.

Kimberly is a high-performing scientist at a biotech company. She takes on any challenge given to her and sees it to completion. However, she is also perceived as being difficult to work with, largely because she becomes easily upset and tends to be passive aggressive with her coworkers.

Her manager and HR contacted me about coaching Kimberly through one specific issue: she was highly stressed out and highly emotional. They told me quite plainly that Kimberly's growth in the company was dependent on her ability to keep her emotions in check. They wanted to see her become more positive, easier to work with, and less reactive.

When I first met with Kimberly, she started crying within the first ten minutes. I tried several approaches to bring her around so we could talk about what she needed to do, but she wasn't hearing me. She simply wanted to vent.

I soon realized that Kimberly's highly emotional state was not the real problem; it was simply the problem people saw. The real problem was that she and her team were overstretched, and taking on responsibilities that weren't theirs in the first place. She was frustrated with this situation but didn't know how to change it, and that showed up in her highly emotional responses.

Had I come in with a five-point plan for controlling one's emotions, I would have been putting a Band-Aid on an issue that went much deeper.

Once we realized what the issue was, we stopped trying to figure out how Kimberly could control her emotions. Instead, we talked about what steps she could take to address the true problem. She started working on two things: setting boundaries and reframing situations so that she saw them differently.

We worked on setting boundaries so that her group was empowered to say no. We worked on influencing and managing her relationships, both her biggest detractors and her friends. We worked on her decision-making process so that she was driven by objectivity more than an emotional attachment to people or processes. We worked on not taking things so personally so that she could see comments about work as not being attacks on her character. We worked on reducing her stress levels by reducing the time she spent stuck in thinking traps, telling herself stories about her being a failure. Finally, we worked on increasing her leadership skills. Soon, Kimberly moved out of survival mode into adapting mode. At the same time, perceptions started to shift—both her coworkers' perceptions of Kimberly and Kimberly's perception of herself.

As part of this process, she identified six coworkers who were struggling with similar issues and created a coaching group. And then she created another coaching group and then another. Kimberly was already overwhelmed, but taking on the work of helping others gave her fulfillment and helped her in the process. She became a much more efficient and effective leader, not by working on reducing her emotional response, but by transforming herself into the person she wanted to be in the first place. When Kimberly started coaching others, she moved into thriving mode and saw real transformational change.

About a year after we started meeting, the company underwent a major reorganization. Kimberly was identified as a high-value employee and is now running one of the key groups of the research organization.

To build resilience and effect transformational change, we have to solve for the real problem, not the perceived problem. For Kimberly, the problem wasn't that she was too emotional. It was the lack of boundaries and resulting perceived helplessness, which led her to become emotional in highly stressful situations.

Kimberly had to accept the way people saw her and that she needed to adapt the behaviors that brought out the side of her that she didn't want in the first place. After accepting where she was at the moment, including the perception of others, Kimberly could envision a different future and start executing the steps to get there.

FOCUS ON THE SYSTEM

Solving for the right problem is just one of the two steps required to create transformational change. We must also focus on the system instead of the goal. It's important to envision an aspirational goal, as that will drive the steps to adapt and thrive. However, if we focus on the goal alone, we miss the benefit of working the system itself—of taking the steps to achieve the goal and enjoying the gradual improvement that happens in the process.

If you are an entrepreneur, for example, your goal might be to build a million-dollar business. Your system is the way you hire, the way you develop and test your ideas, the way you market your product in pursuit of your goal. The goal provides direction; the system allows you to take action and measure progress. Focusing on the system ensures that you improve over time en route to achieving the goal.

When Richard and I started working together, he was very clear on his goal: he wanted to be promoted to vice president. That was his sole focus, and everyone knew it. Everything Richard did was seen as part of his attempt to win that promotion.

As I interviewed people in the organization, the data was pretty strong that Richard needed to make some changes before that promotion could happen. For example, his manager said he was a great performer, but if he wanted to go further, he needed to have a bigger network and more conversations about the company, not necessarily about his job. He needed to show his potential, not just his competence in the present role—his value beyond his current "pay rate."

I presented this feedback to Richard and suggested that, rather than focus on the promotion itself, he work on being the type of person who gets promoted. In other words, I encouraged him to focus on the system—ask for suggestions and feedback, look for opportunities to add value—and not the goal. Once he started working on the things keeping him from the promotion—the skills he needed to improve and leverage and the way he was showing up (or not)—people noticed. (Spoiler alert: Richard eventually got the promotion. Read on to find out how.)

When I was training for my first two Ironman triathlons, I focused on getting to the pool every day. Based on what I had heard, I thought swimming every day was the way to build endurance, so I put in a lot of pool time. If I missed a day, I felt horrible. In the end, I did build endurance, but I still wasn't a great swimmer. I realized that, just as Richard had focused on the promotion instead of the process of becoming promotable, I was focusing on checking off the "time in the pool" box rather than improving my skills and fitness in preparation for the Ironman. I completed the swim portion with no problem, but I also realized that given the amount of time I had spent in the pool, I should have performed better.

On my third Ironman, I took a different approach. I decided to focus on the system rather than the goal of checking off the "I swam today" box. I became more intentional about improving my form and efficiency during each workout, rather than swimming a huge number of laps. As I focused on small improvements, I began to swim better overall and my time improved. I also started to enjoy the pool a lot more because I was looking forward to seeing the improvement.

One of Kimberly's aspirational goals was to set boundaries for herself and her team. To achieve this goal, we worked on smaller steps, the system if you will. Part of her system to achieve this goal involved saying no to three people each day—practical actions to set boundaries. She also created a system for defining which problems were hers to solve. She took intentional steps to start building that boundary muscle. Little victories provide positive reinforcement, which is essential for moving forward and realizing transformational change.

You might be thinking, *This solution sounds too simple.* It is—but it's not easy. For Kimberly, shifting her focus from the goal to the system required to achieve the goal involved courage and persistence. It will likely be the same for you.

CREATE WINNING HABITS

After you figure out your aspirational goal and the process to get there, create winning habits to make it happen. The key to creating habits that stick is to start with the low-hanging fruit.

Habits need to be trained, and we are more likely to continue when we receive rewards for our actions. Start with something small, easily attainable, and safe. After a habit is trained, we can then give it more responsibilities.

When I wanted to start a writing habit, I didn't start with seven hundred words a day. I started with fifty words a day. You might give yourself added motivation by, say, contributing five dollars to the campaign fund of the political candidate you don't support if you miss a day. (Believe me, this works. Out of fifty-three days, I only missed five because I *really* didn't want to support a certain candidate.) After I reached 150 days of writing fifty words a day, I increased my daily total to five hundred words. This habit is now automatic—I actually look forward to getting my words in first thing each morning.

Similarly, when people have several credit cards with unpaid balances, one recommended pay-off method is to pay off the one with the highest balance first. Another well-known strategy, known as the Debt Snowball Method, involves doing the opposite: in other words, start with the card with the lowest balance—the one you can pay right away. Once that small balance is paid you can focus on the account with the next smallest balance, and so on—like a snowball, you gain momentum with each small win because you have more money to pay off the next one more quickly, and those paid accounts build up your motivation to keep paying off debt. Grabbing that low-hanging fruit can be a huge motivator to pay off the next, and the next.[17]

---

17 Ramsey Solutions, "How the Debt Snowball Method Works," Ramsey, July 14, 2022, https://www.ramseysolutions.com/debt/how-the-debt-snowball-method-works.

Remember: Forming habits is a process. It doesn't happen overnight. Here are two habit-creation methods to get you started.

KEYSTONE HABIT

In his book *The Power of Habit,* Charles Duhigg discusses a shift that took place in Alcoa, an aluminum company that was struggling in the 1980s. When they brought in a new CEO, Paul O'Neill, people had high hopes that he was going to change strategies and processes and turn the company around.

At the first meeting with the stakeholders, O'Neill started by saying, "Let's talk about employee safety." People freaked out. The company was losing market capability and money, but he wanted to talk about employee safety—not profit margins, revenue projections, cost savings, or anything else that would be comforting to Wall Street ears. But O'Neill was adamant. "I intend to make Alcoa the safest company in America, I intend to go for zero injuries."[18]

Investors ran out of the room. One sprinted to a payphone and called his twenty largest clients and advised them to sell their stock immediately: "The board put a crazy hippie in charge, and he is going to kill the company."[19]

From that moment on, every person at every level of the organization started making decisions through the lens of employee safety. And it worked. During O'Neill's tenure, Alcoa's worker injury rate dropped dramatically. In addition, product quality started improving along with the focus on

---

18 Charles Duhigg, *The Power of Habit: Why We Do What We Do in Life and Business* (New York: Random House, 2012), 200 (e-book).

19 Duhigg, *Power of Habit*, 202.

employee safety, and over time Alcoa experienced a substantial turnaround. When O'Neill took over, Alcoa was worth millions; when he left, it was worth billions.

By focusing on the particular metric of employee safety, Alcoa's CEO created change that rippled through the whole organization. Duhigg refers to this change agent as a *keystone habit*—the one habit that will influence everything else. As O'Neill explains, "I knew I had to transform Alcoa. But you can't order people to change. So I decided I was going to start by focusing on one thing. If I could start disrupting the habits around one thing, it would spread throughout the entire company."[20]

After I was diagnosed with the brain tumor, I took on running as a keystone habit because it was something I could control. The more I ran, the more my running improved. After I trained for and ran the Chicago Marathon with my wife, I started to raise the bar. I ran a few marathons, then tackled my first 50K. After I ran a few more 50Ks, I did a 50 Miler, a 100K, and finally a 100-mile ultramarathon. With each race, I gained confidence, which spilled over into other areas, particularly in tackling difficult tasks. In addition, I started improving other life skills, especially in the area of relationship building. Through my running habit, I met future business partners, as well as Rujeko, my second wife.

A keystone habit can be the catalyst for positive changes in many other areas of your life, the habit that influences everything else.

---

20 Duhigg, *Power of Habit*, 204.

ATOMIC HABITS

In his book *Atomic Habits*, James Clear defines an atomic habit as a regular practice or routine that is not only small and easy to do, but also has the power of compound growth. In other words, the more atomic habits you form, the more growth you enjoy.

In a sense, atomic habits are the small actions that support the bigger keystone habit. Running was my keystone habit, but I developed atomic habits such as daily pushups and better eating by cooking my own meals, which supported my running habit.

When I was working with Kimberly, I suggested that she form the keystone habit of curiosity. By engaging with others with curiosity as a repeatable and deliberate behavior, she started developing other positive qualities, particularly mindfulness, empathy, humility, and a learning mindset. Being curious also sent the signal to her coworkers that she was flexible, collaborative, and open to being influenced—things that people wanted to see from her more often.

To work on curiosity, I encouraged Kimberly to develop several atomic habits. For example, she focused on asking specific questions such as "Why?" "What if...?" and "How might we...?" The more she used these questions intentionally to strengthen her keystone habit of curiosity, the more she experienced real transformational change in other areas: she made fewer decision-making errors, experienced reduced conflict with coworkers, and enjoyed more open communication.

Bad habits repeat themselves because we don't have a system to replace them. Changes that seem small at first turn into remarkable results if we are willing to stick with them and make them a part of our everyday operating system.

A NEW MANTRA

To adapt and eventually thrive, sometimes we have to do stuff that isn't pleasant. The military uses the phrase "embrace the suck"—consciously accept and appreciate something that is unpleasant but unavoidable.

Embracing the suck is the initial step toward moving out of survival mode. If you can accept your situation as it is, you give yourself space to ask the key question: *what am I going to do about it?* Let this be your new mantra in the face of every change and hardship. Then envision the possibilities and take the first step to make it happen.

One of the most common reasons we get stuck in survival mode is fear: fear of rejection, fear of failure, fear of all the unknown "what ifs" and "what abouts." The second pillar will help you face your fears rather than hide from them.

RECAP: EMBRACE THE SUCK

Where you are now is the place you need to be, no matter what that looks like. The key is not wishing for more, but rather doing the best with what is available. Embrace the suck and move forward, one step at a time.

Accept

Radical self-acceptance isn't an excuse to become complacent and accept the status quo. Consciously accepting and appreciating who you are right now allows you to choose what to do next.

What have you been struggling to accept about yourself?

Envision

Michelangelo is attributed with warning that danger lies in aiming too low, not from aiming too high.

What do you really want to achieve? Aim for the skies.

Execute

Don't focus on the problems you cannot solve; focus on what is in your control.

What problem are you currently facing that is yours to solve? What is your first step?

Chapter 5

FACE YOUR FEARS

Don't aim to be fearless. Aim to fear less.

- *Welcome* fear.
- *Challenge* your relationship with fear.
- *Act* because of your fear.

Prior to my tumor diagnosis and surgery, I had started swimming with the Michigan State triathlon team and competed in some sprint-length triathlons. With a few sprints under my belt, I signed up for an Olympic-length race and then a half Ironman.[21] With each race and each increase in distance, I faced the same fears: *Will I be able to do this? Am I*

---

21 A sprint-length triathlon consists of a half- mile (750-meter) swim, 12.4-mile (20-kilometer) bike ride, and 3.1-mile (5-kilometer) run. Olympic length involves a .93-mile (1.5-kilometer) swim, 24.85-mile (40-kilometer) bike ride, and 6.2-mile (10-kilometer) run. The half Ironman, also known as the Ironman 70.3 in reference to the total number of miles, consists of a 1.2-mile (1.9-kilometer) swim, 56-mile (90-kilometer) bike ride, and 13.1-mile (21.1-kilometer) run.

good enough? Though nervous until the starting gun fired, I pressed through because of my overwhelming desire to get better and to prove to myself that I could do more.

Then, in 2005, I signed up for a full Ironman, a grueling 140.6-mile race consisting of a 2.4-mile (3.9-kilometer) swim, 112-mile (180-kilometer) bike ride, and 26.2-mile (40.1-kilometer) run. Again, I was filled with fear that despite my extensive training, I wouldn't be able to finish. Plus, the swimming portion took place in the ocean in Panama City Beach, Florida, and I had never competed in an open water swim.

For moral support in my endeavor, I asked one of my friends from the Michigan State triathlon team to compete with me. Ken and I arrived in Panama City Beach two days before the event. We drove the run and bike portions of the course and, most importantly, tested the water.

As soon as I jumped in during our test swim, I swallowed a huge gulp of salt water and almost puked. *What have I gotten myself into?* I thought. The water on the test day was warm, but the weather report showed it might be windy and cooler on the day of the race. If it were cold enough, we would be able to wear wetsuits during the swim, which would increase my buoyancy and make the swim easier. I prayed for cooler weather.

I don't remember much from those two days of preparation, other than I was heart-pumping, I'm-going-to-die-out-there scared. Ken, on the other hand, was excited. It was his first Ironman, too, but he was in much better shape and was looking forward to the challenge.

The day of the event, I was petrified. After breakfast, which I barely ate, we went to the transition area where we had dropped off our bikes and gear the day before. I stopped short when I saw my bike: it had a flat tire. As I frantically tried to figure out how to change the tire, I heard the organizers tell participants to make their way to the starting line. My hands trembled as I worked, and I started thinking that this might be a good excuse for me to drop out. *I can always say that mechanical problems forced me to abandon the race.*

By the time I finished fixing the tire, I was nearly alone. The temperature had dropped enough that we were able to wear wetsuits, so I quickly put mine on. As I hurried toward the starting line, I thought of Aaron, a legally blind triathlete I had met during my time training at Michigan State. He had once told me, "Luis, we don't have to be scared all the time. Let's just go out there and have fun."

When I arrived at the beach and saw the sea of people—all two thousand of them—I felt the weight of what I was about to do. I joined the crowd, and soon found myself being pushed toward the water as the people around me started moving forward. I panicked a little and started talking to myself: *I'll be okay. I'll be okay.* Finally, we stopped moving and we all waited, shoulder to shoulder.

At one point, I turned around and saw a woman near me crying.

"Are you okay?" I asked.

"This is so emotional," she said. "I can't wait to get started."

You're so full of it, I thought. She was just as scared as I was. I could see it on her face. In fact, I realized, I could see it on many participants' faces, that look of, *Oh my gosh. What am I doing?!*

As I anxiously waited for the start, I couldn't help but overhear the comments of those pressed around me: "Oh my, the wind just came up." "Look at those whitecaps." "It's so choppy!"

I hadn't noticed the water until I heard people talking about it, and their words increased my fears. I suddenly felt queasy.

I glanced to my left and saw two people puking. Then I had another thought: *I'm not alone!* That gave me a little courage.

When the gun went off, I waited for the crowd in front of me to move and then sprinted toward the water, all while trying not to get trampled. As I ran, an amazing thing happened. My fear simply disappeared.

I felt my feet hit the water, and I kept running until it became too deep to run. Then I started swimming. It was a mad jumble of bodies and arms and legs. Once I hit the first buoy, the crowd thinned out, and I settled into a groove.

After two laps around the triangular course, I finished the swim portion; I didn't die like I had feared. I also finished the bike and run portions, though the bike portion in particular was brutal because of the wind. When I was finally able to see the finish line, I decided to enjoy the moment. I high-fived people lined up along the course, and as I crossed under the finish banner, I held a sign high above my head that said, "Sara, I love you."

I've competed in nine Ironman distance competitions since my first in Panama City, and each time I have the same experience. I'm not as nervous as I was the first time, but I'm still scared right up to the point when I start running toward the water, and then my fear simply fades away.

This experience has greatly influenced the way I think about and coach clients around fear. First, it's helpful to know we're not alone. Seeing the expressions on my fellow participants' faces gave me courage to continue, knowing I wasn't the only one feeling scared. The same holds true in the workplace and in life in general. When we are willing to be vulnerable about the challenges we face, we find others who are afraid of the same situations and circumstances. There's a bond in mutually shared struggles.

Second, I learned that fear shouldn't keep me from participating in the things that scare me. In fact, the best way to approach something I'm fearful of is to do it anyway. Now I am very intentional about doing things that cause fear. The goal isn't to be fearless but to fear less, and this only happens as we consciously take action in the face of our fears.

Finally, after I completed my first Ironman, I took time to evaluate what I learned and how I could do better the next time. I have applied these lessons to each Ironman I've done since, and I encourage my clients to do the same with whatever situation they're facing.

The goal isn't to deny fear or pretend it doesn't exist. Neither is the goal to become fearless, for fearless individuals are reckless and set themselves up for disappointment and failure. Instead, we want to learn how to welcome fear, challenge our relationship with it, and ultimately act even when we feel it. As we go through this process with different fears, we will become more comfortable in those arenas and our fears will decrease. As this happens, it is important to intentionally explore what we did so we can do it again the next time around.

WELCOME FEAR

The first step in facing our fear is to welcome it. In essence, we welcome fear by acknowledging that we're afraid—by feeling the emotion, by making room for that fearful response. In admitting our fear, we open the door to figuring out how to act in spite of it.

It's easier to welcome fear and thus face it if we can identify what we're afraid of.

TYPES OF FEAR

In a *Psychology Today* article titled "The (Only) 5 Fears We All Share," Dr. Karl Albrecht explained that every fear humans experience—whether we are afraid of being bitten by a dog, turned down for a promotion or date, or even getting our taxes audited—generates a standardized biological reaction and can be fit into one of five overarching categories:[22]

- *Fear of extinction*: Dr. Albrecht makes a distinction between the final loss of life and the loss of everything you enjoy in that life. The fear of extinction is the fear of ceasing to exist, of no longer being who you are and no longer being around to enjoy your life and all the people in it.
- *Fear of mutilation*: Dr. Albrecht equates fear of mutilation with fear of bodily invasion by illness or disease or loss of limb.
- *Fear of loss of autonomy*: This fear is related to a fear of being restricted, suffocated, or becoming completely dependent on others. When I underwent surgery, I feared I would end up paralyzed or, worse, a vegetable.
- *Fear of separation*: At its core, fear of separation is the fear of abandonment, rejection, or loss of connectedness—a fear of being unwanted, not respected, or not valued by another person. For me, this fear showed up after my brain surgery, when I was no longer able to perform my duties as a professor. I feared being left behind because I could no longer keep up with everyone else.
- *Fear of ego-death*: Dr. Albrecht groups fear of humiliation with fear of shame and feeling worthless. After my surgery,

---

[22] Karl Albrecht, "The (Only) 5 Fears We All Share," *Psychology Today*, March 22, 2012, https://www.psychologytoday.com/us/blog/brainsnacks/201203/the-only-5-fears-we-all-share.

for example, I was afraid of not being the person I was before and the shame this made me feel. I used to be smart, but now I couldn't even remember my phone number.

These fears show up in everyday life, including in the workplace. In the leaders I coach, I have seen variations of these five basic fears played out in many different ways. Do any of these sound familiar?

- *Fear of failure*: Even the strongest, most intelligent, most competent leaders fear failure. Self-confidence works when you're on a winning streak, but when you have setbacks, confidence quickly diminishes. As a leader, you're likely not afraid of physically dying on a day-to-day basis, but you might be afraid of failing in your new role. If you think you will fail and lower your expectations to cope with it, you destroy your imagination and your ability to envision a future beyond the current crisis. Fear of failure can lead you to focus on succeeding at all costs or find a way out, perhaps blaming others or circumstances to avoid being attached to such failure. Ahead of my first Ironman, fear of failure caused me to look for excuses why I wouldn't succeed, for example, the mechanical issues with my bike.
- *Fear of succeeding*: This is the other side of the fear of failure. You might know you have the skills and could succeed in a new role, but fear you won't be able to maintain that success and stay there. Or you might fear the consequences of succeeding: the increased responsibility or the need to manage more people or the implications that success might have on your home life. These fears can cause you to sabotage yourself and block your path to attaining the promotion.

- *Fear of being left behind*: High-potential leaders who are repeatedly passed over for promotion, or who tend to self-sabotage, experience this fear. This fear showed up in Richard, the client mentioned in Chapter 4 who was singularly focused on being promoted. He feared being left behind, and it showed up as constantly "running for office" and trying to get attention. He wasn't trying to show off his skills so much as he was afraid of being left behind.
- *Fear of criticism*: This fear also falls into the "fear of humiliation" bucket. It is rooted in a fear of what people think of you, but it is dangerous to assume you know what those thoughts are. This often happens when you avoid asking for feedback on your impact and instead try to guess what your boss is thinking. Doing so can cause you to make up stories and then make decisions based on them, which most often doesn't serve you well.
- *Fear of making a mistake*: Whereas fear of failure is a comment on the person overall, fear of making a mistake is related to a single task. People who fear making mistakes are often perfectionists, and their fear can lead to defensiveness, self-justification, and lots of anxiety. This happened to Cesar, a client who spent excessive time preparing documents and refused to accept help or show progress until he thought it was ready. The fear of making a mistake led Cesar to put unnecessary pressure on himself and resulted in unnecessary stress.
- *Fear of becoming irrelevant*: This particular fear is common among successful people who have achieved an expert position, and then focus all of their energy on keeping that position, believing that without that position, their opinions won't matter and they may be replaced. This fear

is a primary reason why people don't delegate: they are afraid that if they do, they will become irrelevant because someone else is essentially doing their job. It also shows up when they prevent others with similar skills from shining, sometimes even blocking the hiring of people who could become a threat.

- *Fear of being an imposter*: Many leaders fear learning they are not as good as they think they are, or worse, they are not as good as *others* think they are. They worry people will find out that their skills or competencies or experiences are less than what they claim. If they receive a promotion or move into a different role, they fear people finding out they're not good enough. Instead of acknowledging their capabilities as well as their hard work, they often attribute accomplishments to external or transient causes, such as luck, good timing, or effort that they cannot regularly expend.

These fears are tied together, and they are not mutually exclusive. If you're afraid of being criticized, you're likely also afraid of being an imposter and making mistakes. You might fear getting fired if you make a mistake or that if you make a mistake, you'll become irrelevant.

Every leader experiences fears like these, so you're not alone. Feeling fear and acting anyway is the path to becoming a successful leader.

FEAR IS A GOOD THING

In studying groups of individuals who immigrate to the United States, researchers have found that certain ethnic groups fare better. These groups tend to have three common denominators that individually don't spell success but together allow them to thrive in their new country.[23]

Firstly, there is a pronounced sense of superiority. This is not mere arrogance, but a belief in their potential to excel, which emboldens these individuals to embrace risks. This trait alone can spiral into narcissism, but it is the interaction with the two subsequent traits that refines it into a catalyst for growth and achievement.

Secondly, a layer of insecurity exists within these individuals. Paradoxically, this is where fear nestles in, the fear of not measuring up, which acts as a safeguard against complacency. While they carry a belief in their own superiority, they do not act recklessly on this belief. Instead, they meticulously assess risks and ponder the consequences of failure. Left unchecked, this insecurity might cripple ambition, but when harnessed, it sharpens decision-making and instills a humility that tempers their self-perceived superiority.

The third and pivotal trait is their approach to feedback. This is not merely about seeking affirmation but is a strategic move in playing the long game. It's an acknowledgment that success is not a sprint but a marathon, requiring persistence, adaptability, and a continuous loop of feedback to navigate the long road ahead. This trait alone could lead to an over-reliance on others' opinions, yet when combined with the other two, it transforms fear into tenacity and sustained effort.

In my professional experience, I've observed this triad in action among the most effective leaders. Superiority gives them confidence in their vision, insecurity keeps them grounded, and their relentless pursuit of feedback ensures

---

23 Amy Chua and Jed Rubenfeld, "What Drives Success?" Opinion, *New York Times*, January 25, 2014, https://www.nytimes.com/2014/01/26/opinion/sunday/what-drives-success.html.

they are not blinded by either. They are acutely aware of the risks and consequences, allowing their sense of insecurity to guard them against fearlessness—which can be as dangerous as fear itself. They leverage their fear—the fear of failing, of not being good enough—as a powerful motivator, ensuring they never rest on their laurels or grow too comfortable in their success.

For many of my Silicon Valley clients, 360 assessments have revealed one common finding that connects to the research about thriving ethnic groups: overall, the most successful leaders see themselves as less effective than the people around them do. That level of insecurity allows them to push themselves even harder. These leaders are incredibly smart, they are at the top of the game, and they know what they bring to the table—but they also possess a certain insecurity because everyone in their organization is highly intelligent. They are also open to feedback and are relentless about getting better. In general, these leaders are well aware that there is room to grow, and they have a healthy fear that usually keeps their egos in check.

The leaders who excel are those who play the long game, who understand that the path to achievement is a constant journey of self-evaluation and recalibration. The combination of these three traits—superiority, insecurity, and the pursuit of feedback—grounded in the underlying fear of not being good enough, creates a dynamic that fosters sustained success. Each trait could be a pitfall in its own right, but together, they form the cornerstone of a resilience that is both powerful and nuanced. It is the mastery of this delicate balance that distinguishes truly exceptional leaders.

CHALLENGE YOUR RELATIONSHIP WITH FEAR

Evolutionarily speaking, fear exists to keep us safe. It allows us to run away or fight when we perceive danger. This worked very well when we were living in caves and jungles and were at war with neighboring tribes. Now, however, we usually aren't faced with life-or-death decisions on a regular basis.

Since fear no longer serves as a life-or-death warning system, we have the freedom to examine our fear more closely and challenge our relationships with it. Although fear can serve a positive function, it can also keep us from moving forward and attaining our goals. When we find out what we're really afraid of in any given situation, we can take steps to address it. This section discusses how.

FEAR IS ROOTED IN STORIES

When we make up (and begin to believe) stories in our heads, we can become caught in thinking traps. If we tend toward a victim mentality, we might make up stories that involve blaming others for our situation. These stories often elevate our level of fear. The more we pay attention to our thinking traps, the more afraid we'll be of doing what we need to do.

I still get annual MRIs to monitor my brain tumor. After my last MRI, I was leaving the building when the nurse called and asked if I was free to see the doctor right then rather than two hours later at my scheduled appointment. This nurse and I usually engage in small talk, but she was all business that day. Suddenly, my fear spiked and my brain started creating stories about the results of the MRI—why the doctor wanted to see me right now, and why the nurse was so serious. My heart started pumping and my gut felt queasy.

When I walked into the waiting room, the nurse didn't even

let me sit down. She immediately led me to an exam room. After about five minutes, the doctor walked in with a serious face, and he's not usually that serious. At this point I was freaking out.

After he closed the door, the doctor said, "How are you?"

"I'm doing well. And you?"

"I'm okay." Because of COVID-19, we were both wearing masks, but the doctor's eyes spoke loudly. He put a hand on my shoulder and said, "Luis, I have good news and bad news. Which do you want first?"

"Give me the bad news first."

"I know this is going to be hard. It happens only once in a lifetime. Luis, the bad news is that you're fifty."

"Is that it?" I said, breathing a sigh of relief and finding the humor in his cruel joke. This doctor works with my wife, so we're friends—but still! (The good news was that nothing has changed in my tumor.)

The stories I was telling myself had gotten me worked up into a state of fear. In that case, I had the answer the same day and could put those fears to rest, but it's not always so quick. If you are telling yourself stories about your job performance or what your manager is thinking, you may not get an answer as quickly as I did, and in the meantime, those fears can become paralyzing.

One of the main ways to combat fear is to challenge those stories and cut them short. Breaking the thinking trap is key to figuring out the first step to adapt, thrive, and move forward. You can do that by cultivating a different relationship with fear and implementing a few key strategies.

CULTIVATE A DIFFERENT RELATIONSHIP

Experiencing fear is a given. However, knowing that fear isn't usually serving the preservation purpose it once did, we can reexamine our relationship with it and cultivate a different one.

Rather than react with fight or flight as our ancestors (rightly) did, we can take a step back and analyze the fear. If we don't learn to separate the fear of potential consequences from the fear itself, we will become paralyzed or react with fight or flight.

We need to call the fear the lie that it is. If we let our brains deal with a toxic boss or starting a business in the same way as being chased by someone with a knife, we will always struggle to find courage to take action. Once we get going, we can use it as fuel to change the narrative and move forward.

Unfortunately, the stories we tell ourselves about what we fear are rooted in our biochemistry. In challenging our fears, there isn't a single solution that works in every situation or for every person, but the following steps might help.

1. Acknowledge That Difficult Things Happen

Sometimes this simple acknowledgment alone can be liberating. In addition, it helps to recognize that other people have gone through this same difficult situation and survived. After you admit that what you're experiencing is hard and that you are afraid, find someone else who has already solved this problem and learn from them. This is where self-compassion comes in handy, since it can help us remember that we are not perfect and we can learn how to handle the bad things that happen.

2. Identify Your Thinking Trap

When Rujeko and I were thinking of having children, I was resistant. I worried my tumor might come back, and I didn't want my children growing up fatherless. At the moment, my tumor hadn't returned, but that didn't matter. I kept catastrophizing and imagining the worst possible outcome would happen.

Rujeko and I went back and forth, back and forth. Then one day she said something that completely changed my perspective—both in that situation and in how I have challenged fears since. She said, "Luis, why are you letting the possibility of your death rule the way you live?"

When we are faced with a high-stakes meeting, conflict with a colleague, or taking on a new challenge, it is normal to experience some anxiety. However, when that anxiety takes on a life of its own and creates a debilitating negative spiral that controls our actions, we have fallen into a thinking trap.

Anxiety Canada (anxietycanada.com), a website that is devoted to supporting people who suffer from anxiety, lists a number of these thinking traps. Here are the most common ones I see in my clients:

- *Catastrophizing*: Imagining the worst-case scenario, for example, "I will get fired if I don't get this deal."
- *Mind reading*: Imagining what others are thinking, for example, "I know I won't get this promotion because my manager thinks I am not good enough, so what is the point of even trying?"
- *Fortune telling*: Imagining what the future holds, for example, "I will fail with this new group because I am the only one without a degree in the field."
- *Black-and-white thinking*: Considering only two possible

outcomes, for example, "I will either make the deal or get fired, so I will probably get fired."
- *Overgeneralizing*: Painting all situations with a generalized outcome, for example, "I made an awful presentation to the CEO last month. I never get things right when I present to executive audiences. This always happens to me."
- *Negative filter/focusing on the negative*: Finding the wrong, the negative, the scary, or the unfairness of every situation, while also ignoring the good, for example, "I blew the presentation; they are never going to fund me."

To challenge our relationship with fear, we have to identify the thinking traps that are keeping us in an anxious, fearful state—the stories we are telling ourselves that are not based in reality but still convince us of impending doom.

3. Challenge Your Thinking Trap

We often accept our negative beliefs (especially about ourselves) without questioning them. We simply assume they are true. I assumed that if I had children, they would grow up without a father. Often, however, when we dig deeper and take a more skeptical perspective toward these traps, we find that the assumptions don't hold any water.

In my case, Rujeko was right: I was worrying about something that hadn't happened and might not ever happen, and it was keeping me from enjoying life. When my wife made that comment, I realized that I was trapped in thinking the worst would happen. To challenge this trap, I asked myself, "What evidence is there that this worst-case scenario will occur?" I came up with nothing solid to validate what I was afraid of. As a result, I decided that I would not let my fear of dying get in the way of living, and we pursued having children. Alexis was born in 2014, and in 2018 we were blessed with our second child, Nathan.

As we talked about in the last chapter, we have to embrace the suck and accept a situation as it is before we can see the possibilities and move forward. That "suck" includes our mental traps and worst fears, if they do come to pass.

When I started meeting with Heather, she had the impression that coaching was corrective, that she needed to meet with a coach because she was having issues, and that this was the last step before getting fired. She was wrong. Her manager actually wanted to help Heather elevate her performance and develop her leadership skills. But Heather didn't believe him. Instead, she created the story that her manager made up the part about elevating her performance so Heather would be more receptive to coaching. She also told herself that she was failing at her work and coaching was a way to correct her performance.

Our first step was to change that impression and reframe coaching as something meant to elevate her performance, just as her manager had intended. Then we wrote out what would happen if her worst-possible fear came true and she got fired. Then I asked her, "How can you challenge this fear?"

"I could ask my boss if I'm going to get fired," she said.

"True, but how can you ask that in a different way?" She needed to get a pulse on her performance, but not her worst-case scenario. We started brainstorming ways she could debunk or validate that fear of getting fired without asking directly.

Ultimately, Heather mustered the courage to ask her manager for general feedback on her job performance and to actually believe him when he said she was doing great and needed to work on a few specific things.

Heather was so relieved. Fear had kept her from taking this relatively simple step to challenge her thinking trap, and debunking it proved life-changing. In the past, the fear of getting fired, of not doing enough, consumed her thoughts, to the point of keeping her awake at night. Today, Heather has an array of strategies to disrupt her thinking traps and challenge the stories in her head—for example, by asking clarifying questions instead of walking away with doubts and then making up stories. She recently said, "I am still afraid sometimes, but now I know that the worst-case scenario is one scenario, and there are others." By facing her fear, Heather unlocked her psychological and mental resilience.

Another strategy I used with Heather was to ask what price she would pay for not taking a risk: "What are you going to miss out on if you keep thinking this way, when the evidence points in a different direction?"

After thinking about it, Heather said, "The opportunity to live a balanced life, without fear of getting fired."

For people like Heather, recognizing what they will lose by inaction is a greater motivator than thinking about what they will gain. Researchers at the University of Pennsylvania found that people who focus on *losing* a reward sometimes are more motivated than those who focus on *gaining* one. In the study, where 281 adults were given a goal of taking seven thousand steps per day, the loss-incentive group (those who lost money each time they didn't walk seven thousand steps) met the goal 50 percent more often than the gain-incentive group (those who earned money each time they walked seven thousand steps).[24]

---

[24] Mitesh S. Patel et al., "Framing Financial Incentives to Increase Physical Activity Among Overweight and Obese Adults," *Annals of Internal Medicine*, March 15, 2016, https://www.acpjournals.org/doi/10.7326/M15-1635.

ACT BECAUSE OF FEAR

After we welcome fear and start challenging our relationship with it, we need to act, even though we might still feel afraid. The truth is, fear will always be there, so we can't wait for it to disappear before we act. In fact, if you don't feel fear, you might be too comfortable. If you are too comfortable, you are not growing. The key here is to act with the fear, to use it as a cue to move forward, even if it is a small step to test the water and get comfortable with it.

START WHERE YOU ARE

As is clear by now, one of the foundational truths about resilience is that we all have the ability to take the first step. It's no different with facing your fears. There is a popular saying that goes: "Start where you are, use what you have, do what you can."

As with any challenge, the key to moving beyond your fear is starting where you are. Many times, we get trapped in fear because we focus on the end result, and we feel incapable of getting there. After my first brain surgery, I was unable to walk straight, let alone run. However, focusing on that seemingly huge goal only amplified my fear that I'd never be able to do so. To start moving forward, I needed to focus on where I was and what I could do right now, rather than the end result. I started slowly walking around the block once. Then I started doing it twice a day. Then I increased the number of blocks I walked at one time. Then I increased the speed at which I walked them. I started where I was and I just kept going. It wasn't fast, or easy, but it was progress.

After I had been working with one of my clients for a while, she opened up about one particular issue in her personal life.

Ying is a scientist who had been divorced for about six years. She told me she was afraid she would be alone for the rest of her life, that she would never find the perfect man.

"What do you need to do to find the right reagent combination for a particular experiment to work consistently?" I asked her.

Without hesitation, she said, "I need to experiment and—" She stopped and got quiet for a second. Then she said, "I see what you're trying to tell me."

To let go of her fear of not finding someone perfect, Ying needed to be open to the possibilities and start experimenting.

When I was contracted to help Victor improve his leadership skills, he didn't know where to start. He wanted to increase his scope and felt he possessed the necessary skills, but he focused on the organizational hurdles he felt prevented him from taking action. He feared he would never be able to jump over those obstacles and get to his goal. One of the questions I kept asking him was, "Where are you right now? What can you do today?"

People viewed Victor as aggressive and defensive, which made sense because he was afraid. He was afraid of not being able to show his capabilities, so he was always in "see what I can do" mode. We agreed that there were two ways he could start overcoming this perception and the fear at the root: he could be more vulnerable and ask for help now and then, and he could also own his mistakes. Victor resisted the second step in particular because he didn't want to look bad. He was afraid of losing face and perceived as a less capable leader. After a few sessions it became clear that Victor wasn't willing to put in the work, and the engagement stalled.

A few months later, the vice president of HR approached me about reinitiating my coaching sessions with Victor because he had been put on a performance improvement plan. The company needed his skills and expertise, but the fact that he was so difficult to work with made it impossible for the team to move forward, so he needed to work with me to improve in specific areas or risk being let go. In the performance improvement plan, Victor's manager and the HR business partner identified three elements that Victor needed to change in order to save his job: collaboration, communication, and ownership. The manager also identified ten individuals on the team with whom Victor needed to work; their opinion of Victor and what it was like to work with him was key for him keeping his job (those people didn't know he was on a performance plan). The goal was set for Victor: change the perception of these individuals, or lose your job.

At this point, the fear of extinction kicked in for Victor. He realized he needed to change or risk getting fired, and he also realized these were necessary changes to advance not only in this company, but in any company. This time, he was ready to do the work, starting right where he was.

Victor determined that his first step was to close the relationship gap with people on his team. He let go of his bravado. He started asking for help, asking people what they needed from him, and apologizing when necessary. Though these were simple steps, they weren't easy for him to take. Regardless, he overcame his fear of looking bad by being vulnerable, owned his mistakes, and asked for help. And it worked.

TAKE THE SMALLEST, SAFEST STEP

Any big decision or change is made up of smaller decisions or changes. The same holds true of facing our fears as well. Start with the low-hanging fruit—the smallest, safest step you can take.

With Victor, the smallest step was approaching the people with whom he was most comfortable, so he went to one and asked what he could do to be more collaborative. This person gave him some suggestions, which he applied to his interactions with the whole team. As Victor did so, people's perceptions started to shift. Victor could see it, which encouraged him to do the same with each person on his list. He approached the safest first and asked for feedback and suggestions, and then the next, and the next.

When I interviewed those ten individuals after three months—the time given for his improvement—eight of the ten people on Victor's team said he had made incredible progress in the three areas identified by his manager (collaboration, communication, and ownership). One of the remaining two said things remained the same, but the other said things had become worse. Victor became a little discouraged that he had not made progress with these two, but I encouraged him to focus on the eight who saw change. The truth is, the issue might have been with the other two individuals, not Victor—and that was not his problem to solve.

Remember the low-hanging fruit idea from Chapter 4? The same applies here. Start in the safest place. No matter what your situation or fear, take the first small step. Don't let yourself become more entrenched in a thinking trap. Start moving.

FEEL THE FEAR

Susan Jeffers wrote a book titled *Feel the Fear and Do It Anyway*, which perfectly sums up this step. Feel the fear and take the small step.

Asking for help and apologizing made Victor feel vulnerable and weak at first. He didn't use the word *fear*, but his demeanor clearly communicated that he was afraid of losing face, of being ashamed. I helped him reframe the meaning of *vulnerability*, so that he could see it as a sign of courage and not weakness; according to Brené Brown, who has made a career out of researching vulnerability, shame, and courage, being vulnerable is the most courageous thing one can do.[25] (I have learned that being vulnerable is a way to connect with people. If we are vulnerable, in most cases, people respond by being vulnerable themselves.)

I also helped Victor replace the voices in his head that were asking "What if...": "What if I don't succeed? What if they laugh at me? What if they take advantage of me?" Instead, he started asking himself "How am I going to do this?" "What am I going to say?" We did a bit of role playing so he could practice interacting with the stakeholders in a way that closed the relationship gap. He still felt the fear of being seen as weak, but he learned how to act anyway.

Finally, I helped Victor look at how he was showing up when he entered a group of people. Like many people, Victor felt like he needed to be authentic with others, but for him, authenticity involved being defensive. So, I encouraged him to feel the fear of losing face and show up differently—as someone who is curious and empathetic, not defensive. Soon, this "faked" way of showing up became his new authentic.

GET ADDICTED TO TAKING ACTION

After you've taken the smallest, safest step, evaluate what's different about you. Some people experience a magical, won-

---

[25] Brené Brown, Daring Greatly: *How the Courage to Be Vulnerable Transforms the Way We Live, Love, Parent, and Lead* (New York: Gotham Books, 2012).

derful high. Some people experience a huge sense of relief. I feel excitement that makes me want to take another step.

Kelly is a client who had been struggling trying to manage her team. She was afraid she wasn't doing a good job of helping them grow and cope with the pressure of the work. She also felt overwhelmed and feared that her boss had noticed her inability to manage her team. Kelly was losing a lot of sleep worrying about both situations.

Finally, she asked one of her direct reports, "Do you have a suggestion for how I can be a better manager for you?" Kelly was pleasantly surprised at the honest and practical suggestions she received from that person, so she asked every one of her direct reports the same question. All of the suggestions were actionable and much less complicated than she expected.

Then Kelly asked her boss a version of that question, and again found the answers insightful and useful. Since then, Kelly has developed a habit of asking for feedback. She got addicted to taking this action as a way to improve her relationships and her job performance.

Action is the result of motivation. As we take action, another force comes into play: satisfaction. And satisfaction leads to motivation to take more action. It's a continuous loop that feeds taking more risks and, ultimately, transformational change in our relationship with fear in that particular area.

Self-confidence is a great motivator when you're making progress, and taking tiny steps ensures your continued progress. Use that to your advantage. Celebrate small steps and small victories and let them spur you to bigger steps.

Taking action in the face of fears builds confidence. As mentioned earlier, I have a fear of being rejected. I walked through the strategies presented here and put myself in low-risk situations where I knew I would be rejected, including the McDonald's drive-thru example. I'm still afraid of being rejected, but I know that it won't kill me, and my small steps have increased my confidence and made me hungry to take even more risks. I also know that my default is to be inconspicuous, so every time I enter a new group, I enter with the intention of being supportive and helpful. Intentionality allows me to step out of my comfort zone safely and look for opportunities to add value.

FEAR LESS

When I moved back to the United States in 2007 after I separated from my first wife, I had three goals: fall in love again, get an MBA, run another marathon. I started working on the third goal almost immediately. I was living in the Bay Area, where there are a lot of running events, so I picked the weekend I wanted to race and I started training.

At that point I had run four marathons, but they had all been city courses, so when I signed up for the Mount Diablo Marathon, I pictured aid stations every mile, lots of people along the course, and hundreds of other runners. The name alone should have told me this was a completely different race.

In the weeks before the marathon, I learned that the Mount Diablo course is a steep trail run in the mountains. They don't have aid stations every mile, so I had to buy a couple of bottles to carry my own water. When I told a couple people that I was doing this race, they went on and on about how hard it was. The more I learned, the more afraid I became.

But I still showed up.

When I arrived, there were only twenty-five other runners, and they were all decked out for serious trail running—no color-coordinated shorts and tanks like I was wearing. In addition, I found out there were actually two races: the marathon and a fifty-mile ultramarathon. Both races followed the same course to the top of the mountain and then the marathon veered off partway down.

The course was rough, and it was hot. I struggled up to the turnaround point at the top and then headed back down. I wasn't exactly sure where the ultramarathon course separated from the marathon, so I decided to follow a couple of old-timers. Several brutal miles later, I finally came to an aid station. Since this is a small race, the organizers know almost all of the participants. The woman at the station didn't know me, so she struck up a conversation as I sipped my water.

"Is this your first ultramarathon?" she asked.

"Uh, no," I said, a little confused. "I'm here for the marathon."

"Oh, dear. You missed a turn. To do the marathon you have to go back up and follow the orange ribbons. Or you can just keep going and do the fifty miler."

I couldn't believe it. At this point, the old-timers were long gone and I had no idea where I was going, so I decided to run back up the mountain and continue on the marathon course. I found the orange ribbons and kept running, but I was in so much pain that I ended up using a long stick as a support as I hobbled through the final miles.

In the end, I ran thirty-seven miles that day—my first ultramarathon, since anything over twenty-six miles is considered an ultra—and it was miserable. I *never* wanted to do that again.

Two days later, however, I was online looking for another ultra. Once the reality of what I had accomplished sunk in, despite my fears and discomfort, my attitude shifted and I wanted to do it again and again and again. The following year, I ran more than thirty-two ultramarathons.

Taking risks is uncomfortable, as is challenging your fears.

Both are likely to push you outside your comfort zone, which is a good thing. When we remain in our comfort zone too long, we can become complacent or, worse, defensive because we will try to defend doing what is comfortable. That's why we need to push ourselves beyond the comfort zone into the stretch zone (Figure 5.1). It will feel uncomfortable at first, especially if we push ourselves hard and move beyond stretching into panic. But as you continue challenging yourself, the boundaries of your comfort zone will expand, and so will the boundaries of your stretch zone, so that your panic zone becomes smaller and smaller.

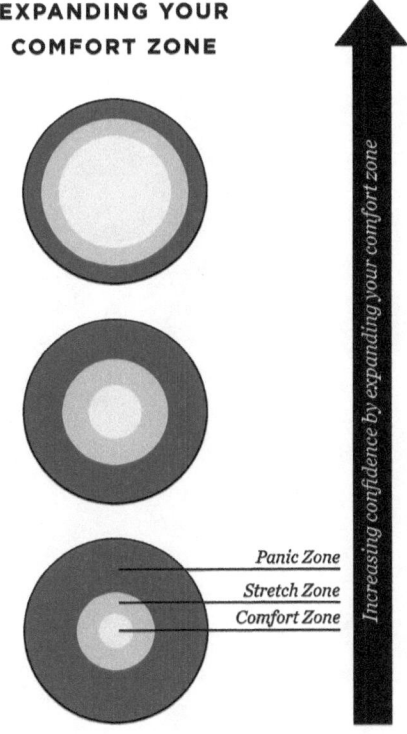

Figure 5.1

As you push the boundaries of your comfort zone in new areas, the fear will still be there. We must use it as a trigger, a motivation, a call to action. We must not reject fear but embrace it, feel it, do the thing we fear anyway. The fears we don't challenge or face become the force that keeps us from moving forward. I think about my fear of dying and how I didn't want my future children to grow up fatherless. That thought kept me from living my dream of becoming a dad. Don't let fear of what could happen make nothing happen.

Next, we will discuss the importance of building relationships with intention and purpose.

RECAP: FACE YOUR FEARS

The goal isn't to deny fear, pretend it doesn't exist, or become fearless. Instead, we want to learn how to welcome fear, challenge our relationship with it, and ultimately act because of it, not despite it.

Welcome Fear

Fear is a good thing. It reminds us we are human.

What exactly are you afraid of?

Challenge Your Relationship with Fear

After you welcome fear, you can use it as a call to action. But first you have to recognize the stories that are feeding your fear and the actions you're avoiding.

What stories are you telling yourself? What are you avoiding?

Act Because of Fear

Feel the fear, whatever it is, and take action anyway.

What is the smallest, safest step you can take today?

Chapter 6

BUILD RELATIONSHIPS

In the dance of life, our partners are the bonds we forge, and with their steps, we find the rhythm to move forward.

- *Identify* the relationships you need to cultivate in your life.
- *Evaluate* the perceptions others have of you and challenge your own perceptions.
- *Engage* people with humility, assertiveness, and empathy.

After Mount Diablo, I became addicted to taking action—to challenging myself through ultramarathons—and in June 2007, I ran a 50K in Pacifica, California. Around halfway into the race, I became aware of one particular runner behind me. Over the miles she kept getting closer, but I was determined that she wouldn't catch me. Then with five miles to go, she passed me. I tried to keep up, but I couldn't.

At my next 50K a few weeks later, this time on Angel Island in San Francisco Bay, I spotted the same runner catching up to me. Once again, around five miles before the end of the race, she passed me. This time we acknowledged each other and exchanged a quick hello before she took off.

After the race, I introduced myself. As we chatted, I learned that Janet viewed me as her private competition, the guy she needed to catch and beat. At my next race, I tried her strategy. I picked a random person in front of me, someone who seemed to be running at a similar pace, and I decided to stay right behind him. Then when the opportunity came, I sped up and passed the person just as Janet had done to me. It worked! I was never going to win an ultra, but I won that little mini competition and I continued to use this strategy at each race, picking a rabbit to chase and hopefully beat.

Janet and I continued to see each other at ultras, and we started running sections together, talking as we ran. Then we started sharing rides to the races and then we started training together, and a close friendship formed. She moved from being a competitor to being my running buddy—not only a running buddy, but also a source of inspiration. She was much more experienced running ultras, and I truly leaned on her for knowledge and inspiration. I even recruited her to help me complete my first one-hundred-mile race in the Moab Desert, in March 2009, and we ran it together.

My next goal was the Western States 100-Mile Endurance Run, the world's oldest 100-mile trail race and also one of the toughest. It starts in Olympic Valley, California, near the site of the 1960 Winter Olympics, and ends 100.12 miles later in Auburn, California.

To have a chance at participating, runners have to run a qualifying time in a different race. Once they do, their name is entered into a lottery, from which 360–400 names are selected out of the thousands of entries. In late 2011, I qualified and my name was drawn, and it was Janet who shared the good news with me.

Most people who run ultramarathons, especially at the one-hundred-mile range, use a pacer. This person's primary job is simply to encourage the runner to keep moving forward. They are a voice of reason when a runner gets stuck in the mental trap of negativity or self-doubt that sometimes accompanies long-distance running. They support the runner when exhaustion and delirium set in, because they do. Pacers have been the lifeline I've needed in many races, the main reason I made it to the finish line. For the Western States 100, I asked Janet to be my pacer. I would run the first sixty miles on my own and then Janet would join me to help with pacing the last forty miles to the finish line.

Janet had already run the Western States, and she shared what she learned. We trained together in preparation for my race, and we planned a nutrition strategy, equipment logistics, and safety. I relied heavily on her expertise to guide me through the process of mentally and physically preparing. I also needed a cheerleader, to keep my confidence up while preparing for the race as well as during the race when the negative Luis would show up.

The race started in Squaw Valley, and Janet was there to help me with the beginning logistics. She met me at various rest stations to make sure I was making good progress. Then, as planned, she joined me at mile sixty and paced me through to the end. After almost twenty-eight hours of continuous running, we entered the high school stadium in Auburn, California, where the race ended. About a half lap before I reached the finish line, Janet veered into the track infield and let me finish all by myself. It was a huge moment.

As I was being congratulated, taking my finisher's picture, sharing that moment with my wife and friends, and high-fiving other finishers, I looked over and saw a crowd hovering over someone on the ground. Janet had collapsed. She had been so busy taking care of me during the last forty grueling miles that she forgot to take care of herself. She was completely depleted and lost consciousness shortly after she let me finish alone. (Don't worry, she made a full recovery.)

That day I learned a lesson I will never forget: how much people are willing to help you if you are willing to ask.

Some of us like to think that we don't need others to get through this life. Some of us might know we need help, but are afraid to ask for it because of the social threats involved, especially at work—the uncertainty, the risk of being rejected, the giving up of autonomy, the risk of losing face and appearing weak or unqualified. In reality, most people are willing to lend a hand if asked; "estimates suggest that as much as 75 to 90 percent of the help coworkers give one another is in response to direct appeals."[26]

The truth is, we cannot do life alone. By nature, we are dependent on others. Whether we like it or not, whether we are aware of it or not, we are the product of the help we have received from others. When I think of the most pivotal moments in my life, I can tie them to specific individuals and the way they helped, challenged, supported, and believed in me when others didn't.

---

26 Heidi Grant, "How to Get the Help You Need," *Harvard Business Review*, May–June 2018, https://hbr.org/2018/05/how-to-get-the-help-you-need.

Relationships are critical to our social and overall resilience; in fact, it is virtually impossible these days to advance in organizations without the collaboration and assistance of others. Yet many of us spend little time deliberately building relationships. I argue that we shouldn't leave something so important to chance. As with every aspect of resilience, we need to be intentional. We need to consciously create connections and form alliances before we need them.

In this chapter, we'll discuss the five key relationships that I encourage my clients to develop, with an eye toward building social resilience.

IDENTIFY RELATIONSHIPS

When I was a kid, my dad used to say, "Tell me who you're hanging out with, and I'll tell you who you are." I didn't realize the wisdom of that statement until I joined a divorce support group and met Daniel.

I had attended a few sessions before I actually talked to Daniel, and it was immediately clear that he was very bitter. He told me how his wife had left him for another man and had taken the kids with her. He was angry that the other man was looking after his children, something that he felt was his right and duty but that his ex-wife prevented him from doing.

"How long were you married?" I asked one day.

"We were married seven years," Daniel replied.

"How long ago did you separate?"

"Ten years ago," he said, apparently still angry.

The more I talked to Daniel, the more I realized that he was stuck in the past. He probably didn't know it, so he kept on living in, as he put it, a miserable situation. I decided I was not going to be like that.

I also decided that this group was full of sad stories, and I needed something different. I needed someone who had already solved my problem, someone who had learned how to move on and find happiness again, someone who could really help me push through my sadness instead of wallowing in it.

When I was a doctoral student at Michigan State, we had "lab meetings" during which graduate students or postdoctoral fellows would talk about the progress they were making on their research. Many times, we ended up talking about the problems and challenges in these projects, and together we would troubleshoot on each person's struggles. It became a support group, if you will, but unlike the divorce support group, our lab meetings focused on finding solutions, rather than sharing horror stories about our experiments. As a group we helped each other consider what we could do differently going forward.

On many occasions, nobody could give a definite solution, but we could offer hunches and articles that covered similar situations. Afterward, the person with the problem took responsibility for looking up the research, considering the proposed idea, and integrating the advice provided, and in many cases, it was enough to move the project past the roadblock.

We all need to be strategic about the relationships we develop, for they play a big role in helping us adapt and thrive in hardship. Social resilience is built when we foster, engage in, and sustain positive relationships that enable us to embrace the suck and move forward. Social resilience is more than fulfilling friendships and the comfortable exchange of ideas. It is not merely warm hugs, unconditional positive regard, or expression of anti-competition sentiments. It is a network of relationships that provide diverse perspectives. Socially resilient people who have built strategic relationships recognize the fact that many tasks require the coordination of people with different backgrounds, values, and priorities. Imagine a professional football team composed of individuals with the same identical skills. That team would have little chance of success. Social resilience implies not merely the acceptance of others, but rather the intentional incorporation of diverse perspectives and skills so we can all learn, adapt, and thrive.

Forming any one of the following relationships will have a positive impact, but the true value is in developing all five. As with the physical, mental, social, and spiritual components of resilience, these five connections have an additive value; together they provide a strong support system and improve your resilience.

MENTOR

At the heart, mentoring is the knowledge transfer from a more experienced individual to someone who is seeking to learn and grow. Having a mentor is incredibly powerful, not only for your career but for life in general.

After my surgery forced me to leave my career as a professor, I transitioned into HR and then into coaching. I looked for coaching certification programs, but none appealed to me. I needed a more practical approach to learning.

I started watching people whom I respected in the field, and I deliberately formed relationships with a few of them, including Frank Wagner and the late Gary Ranker. I didn't explicitly ask them to mentor me, but that was my intention. Once my relationships with both individuals had been established, I started asking coaching-related questions, such as, "I've been thinking about... What do you think?" and "This is the approach I'm planning to take. Can you help me figure this out?" Then they shared their knowledge.

We often spend a lot of time solving problems when we should be mimicking solutions. In searching out mentors, we should look for people who naturally fill in the gaps in our learning. In my case, mentors shared ideas and practices from which I learned and then developed my own style of coaching.

SPONSOR

A mentor can provide valuable assistance, but I believe you can't thrive in your career or in life without a sponsor. Whereas a mentor shares ideas and then lets the mentee implement them, a sponsor is more actively involved in helping and advocating.

After I graduated from high school, I started looking for work to support my family. I applied at several places, including a nonprofit where a distant cousin of my father worked.

Although I didn't get the job, this individual took it upon himself to advocate for me. He introduced me to the Scholarship for Peace program and guided me through each step of the application process. He told me what to fill out, where to send it, what test to take, when to take it, and so much more. It's ultimately his sponsorship that put me in a place to win the scholarship that brought me to the United States.

When I arrived in California at the age of seventeen, I had never traveled outside Guatemala, and I didn't know any English. At the Fresno airport, I was greeted by my host family for the next year, Bob and Wilma. This older couple adopted me into their family. They took me to my first football game, to Yosemite, and to the Rose Parade in Pasadena. They treated me like a son and made it possible for me to attend community college and learn English, which set the foundation for a thirst for learning that would become an obsession. Bob and

Wilma became sponsors who played an important role in how I adapted and thrived in my new environment.

In a work setting, having a career sponsor is critical if you want to advance. What you've likely heard is true: it is not just about what you know, but who you know and, most importantly, who knows you. Many decisions will be made about your career when you are not in the room. A sponsor can position you and advocate for you behind the scenes. Whereas a mentor's value is seen when you are with him or her, a sponsor's value happens when you are not present.

A sponsor relationship often comes about as you help that person solve a problem. Many years ago, a young analyst helped Barry Diller, a well-known American businessman, prepare data for an acquisition.[27] Diller became fond of the young man and started relying on him more often. Diller also positioned the young man for growth and success, eventually making him the CEO of Expedia, one of his acquired companies. This analyst, Dara Khosrowshahi, is currently the CEO of Uber, and has said he wouldn't have risen to where he is without Diller. That's the power a sponsor can have on someone's career.

PARTNER

The wingman or partner is a symbiotic relationship built on mutual trust and a shared drive to succeed. Both people in this alliance realize they are better together.

In a relationship with a mentor or sponsor, you are largely

---

[27] Dara Khosrowshahi, interview by Lepi Jha Fishman, Stanford Graduate School of Business, December 3, 2018, https://www.youtube.com/watch?v=M8aCKi3dsVg&ab_channel=StanfordGraduateSchoolofBusiness.

the recipient of information and other benefits. You are there to learn. With a partner, you and the other individual both enter the relationship with an understanding that you're together for the ride, that you will both benefit from each other's efforts.

As such, partners are supportive, open, protective, trusting, and also very honest. They tell it like it is without being afraid of hurting the other person's feelings. Candid comments, feedback, and suggestions come from a place of wanting each other to grow.

A true partner can help in many different ways—for example, they can be a "sounding board." When we're in the midst of a situation, it's hard to disassociate ourselves and remain objective. In these situations, it's helpful to have someone on the outside give us a fresh perspective.

A partner can also act as someone who amplifies your message. The best way to advocate for yourself is to have others do it for you. The partner can bring to light all that you're doing, and you can do the same for them. In his book *Give and Take*, Wharton professor Adam Grant points out that it is easier to advocate for others than for ourselves, and that when we do, we are perceived as more assertive, which elevates our standing in the eyes of others, along with those for whom we're advocating.

The women in President Obama's administration demonstrated this aspect of partnership through their "amplification strategy."[28] When one woman made a key point, the others repeated it, giving credit to its author. In advocating for and

---

28 Juliet Eilperin, "White House Women Want to Be in the Room Where It Happens," *Washington Post*, September 13, 2016, https://www.washingtonpost.com/news/powerpost/wp/2016/09/13/white-house-women-are-now-in-the-room-where-it-happens/.

amplifying the voice of another, these women also made room for themselves by speaking up and showing themselves assertive. What a brilliant and simple way to support and elevate others, while elevating themselves at the same time.

I have several partners, one being Janet, my running buddy, and another being Wai, a fellow executive coach. Wai and I look out for each other. He told me about a job opportunity at Stanford, and now we are both leadership facilitators there. For a while we met every week, just to check in on each other and help each other, particularly around business development, positioning, and elevating our brand. This relationship has paid tremendous dividends for me, particularly in terms of how I win business. With Wai's help, I took apart how I approached my first meeting with potential clients to see how I could get better at it. We practice new interview techniques with each other, and we have both seen positive results in our practice. I can honestly say that without Wai's partnership, I wouldn't have experienced the success I have as a coach. And he tells me that our partnership has helped elevate the confidence he has as a coach. A definite win-win.

When Wai and I meet, we make sure we show up in a way that is most helpful to the other person in that particular moment. For example, I might bring up a subject and Wai will ask me, "How do you want me to respond? Do you need advice, coaching, a sounding board, or just an outlet to vent?" Because we have an explicit agreement to show up in a way that best helps the other person, our conversations are more productive. We are friends, but our stated goal as partners is to help each other elevate our brands and offer support in whatever way it's needed.

In terms of building social and overall resilience, the partner is indispensable. A partner can help you regain perspective when you are discouraged or stuck. They can remind you to break the thinking traps, challenge your fears, and reframe a challenging situation. They can advocate for you—and you can do the same for them.

MENTEE

If you truly want to master something, the best way is to teach it to someone else. That is the essence of the mentee relationship.

A few years ago, I had drinks with a friend, and he brought along Curt, who was a successful executive in Silicon Valley who was in the process of exploring a new career in coaching. I gave Curt a few pointers regarding classes to take, coaching certifications to obtain, and books to read. I also gave him my contact information and told him to reach out if he needed anything.

A few weeks later, Curt called with some follow-up questions. I gave him some information, and he soon came back for more help. We ended up meeting weekly to discuss his challenges in starting his transition. To make it easier for me to explain the business of coaching, I created a quick PowerPoint presentation called "The Business of Coaching." In the process, I clarified for myself what was working in my business and what was not. As a result, I created a business roadmap that has improved since the first time I used it with Curt. The PowerPoint I created for Curt ended up becoming a solid training manual for new coaches and the foundation of my own business strategy.

This relationship helped me as much as it helped Curt. As we kept talking and meeting, we discovered synergies and complementing skills, and we became very good friends. The relationship moved from mentor-mentee to a partnership, as Curt is now officially a business partner. In both stages, as a mentor and later as a partner, I have been the recipient of many benefits.

By having a mentee, you not only help someone increase their skills, you can also gain new visibility within the organization. This relationship also helps the mentor improve leadership skills. Companies are always looking for employees who are leaders, who can scale their leadership and teach others and who can pass on organizational knowledge quickly.

In Chapter 4 I mentioned Richard, my client who had been focused on being promoted instead of making himself the kind of person who is promoted. Our conversations took place around the time George Floyd was killed in May 2020. Richard is African American and he was understandably angered by the incident, so we talked about how he could use that energy to help others.

Richard had noticed that there weren't many African American leaders at his level in the company, so he started mentoring some of the up-and-coming African American employees for the purpose of helping them grow and eventually get promoted faster. In the end, one of the reasons Richard was promoted was because the people above him saw how he was adding value to those employees and to the company as a whole.

If growing your career is your goal, becoming a mentor makes you a greater asset to the organization. Employers are looking for leaders who can articulate their message, scale their leadership, and transfer their knowledge. Mentoring someone can also lead to you learning new skills (reverse mentoring) or even gaining a personal alliance that might pay some hefty dividends down the road.

Leaders help others, elevate others, and invest in others. They don't do it because it's their job, but because they want to. Finding a mentee signals to others that you have this desirable quality. A side benefit is that you are able to grow in experience, confidence, and knowledge as you mentor.

COMPETITOR

The business world is full of rivalries—think of Steve Jobs versus Bill Gates and Jeff Bezos versus Elon Musk—and some of these rivalries have resulted in amazing breakthroughs. Having a partner at work will accelerate your growth and your brand, but so can having a competitor—if the competition is implemented the right way.

With competitors, we are naturally in a win-lose situation, whether the competition is a sporting event or a battle for resources in an organization. But does it have to be this way? Why can't we simply make the pie bigger—a win-win situation—so the competitor is less of an adversary and more of a potential partner? A *Harvard Business Review* article found that competition where people stood to lose something created anxiety and negative results, whereas competition where people stood to win something drew excitement.[29] Healthy competition can lead to big wins for all.

If you view a competitor from a win-win mindset, you might see what they're doing, learn from it, and adapt it somewhere else. From this perspective, the problem you're trying to solve is not the competitor themselves but the issue you're

---

29 Anna Steinhage, Dan Cable, and Duncan Wardley, "The Pros and Cons of Competition among Employees," March 20, 2017, https://hbr.org/2017/03/the-pros-and-cons-of-competition-among-employees.

both tackling. In a win-lose situation, however, you might see what the competitor's doing and try to take it from them.

People who function from a scarcity mindset tend to think in terms of win-lose because they don't think there's enough to go around. According to Stephen Covey, author of *The 7 Habits of Highly Effective People*, people with a scarcity mentality view life as a finite pie, so that if one person takes a big piece, that leaves less for everyone else. Covey describes the scarcity mentality as "the zero-sum paradigm of life. People with a scarcity mentality have a very difficult time sharing recognition and credit, power, or profit—even with those who are supposed to be on the same team. They also have a very hard time being genuinely happy for the success of other people."[30] Many people, particularly in the corporate world, have been conditioned to have this kind of scarcity mentality.

Covey also talks about the abundance mentality, which sees that there is plenty out there, enough to spare for everyone. This mindset leads to healthy competition. It allows us to be more compassionate, to share resources and recognition, and to celebrate others' successes.

Though you might adopt an abundance mindset and view a competitor as a potential ally or partner, you cannot control how the competitor sees you. Even if the other person approaches your relationship with a win-lose mentality, you can still act in a way that prioritizes the relationship and appreciates their point of view. As you listen with greater depth, express yourself with more courage, and remain nondefensive, chances are the competitor will begin to realize you really do want a win-win for both of you. When that happens, you have turned that person into a potential ally/partner.

---

30 Stephen Covey, *The 7 Habits of Highly Effective People* (New York: Simon and Schuster, 2004), 378.

If you focus on doing your best, the competition will take care of itself. If you are competing with other people, that becomes the target. And if defeating the competition becomes the goal, you lose track of the problem you were trying to solve in the first place.

The key to this relationship is how you view the competitor. Are you solving for the competition or for the issue you both want to solve?

EVALUATE PERCEPTIONS

One of the most important components of navigating work, entrepreneurship, and relationships, wherever they form, is having courage. And the most courageous thing we can do is see ourselves as others see us, even when others' perceptions don't match our own. Risking the possibility that others don't see us as the capable individuals we think we are requires a lot of courage.

The evaluation component is not so much about evaluating others or finding the right person, but about examining how you show up in the world and what assumptions people might be making about you. The other side of that coin is evaluating and challenging whatever assumptions you are making about yourself and others.

Daniel, a coaching client of mine, was successful, driven, and hungry to succeed even more than he already had. He had been identified as "high potential" and groomed to get promoted. However, he hadn't moved up yet, and he had been on that "high potential" list longer than others who had already been promoted.

After interviewing Daniel, his manager, his direct reports, and his team members, it became obvious that his issue wasn't technical. It was that he was oblivious to, or refused to acknowledge, the needs and wants of others, including his direct reports. Daniel met or exceeded his numbers every quarter, but his team was unhappy, so unhappy that many people had already quit or transferred, or they wanted out. Daniel seemed to think that since he was consistently performing well, this problem with his team wasn't a problem. Daniel was, for all intents and purposes, "a brilliant jerk."

According to a Gallup poll, only one in ten supervisors has the innate ability to lead,[31] and Daniel appeared to be one of those who lacked it, mainly because of his lack of awareness toward his team. He could not see, or chose to ignore, the lack of engagement being caused by his behavior.

According to the late Gary Ranker, one of my mentors and author of *Global Mindset Leadership*, we need to gain awareness on three levels. As we take steps to know ourselves and others in these ways, our emotional intelligence grows, and we grow as leaders.

1. *Self-awareness*: How well do you know yourself? What are your strengths and weaknesses? In what conditions do you thrive? What have your life experiences taught you? It has been documented that people who overestimate their abilities have a somewhat harder time accomplishing their goals. The opposite is also true: people who underestimate their abilities, or appear to do so, tend to rank high in leader performance. Jack Zenger and Joseph Folkman explain this phenomenon in a *Harvard Business Review* article and deduce that those who underrate themselves

---

[31] Amy Adkins, "Only One in 10 People Possess the Talent to Manage," Gallup, April 13, 2015, https://www.gallup.com/workplace/236579/one-people-possess-talent-manage.aspx.

tend to have a rare combination of humility and high personal standards, and continually strive to be better.[32] And that is the key: self-aware individuals know themselves, and are also on a quest to improve as a result of what they learn about themselves.

2. *Social awareness*: What are the rules, written and unwritten, in this environment? What is the culture—a culture of feedback? a culture of coaching? a culture of punishment? What are people's aspirations, goals, fears, and concerns? Social awareness involves being able to read the room and the people in it. It allows us to develop empathy by understanding other people's feelings, wants, and needs and then take an active interest in meeting them. Second, when we read the room and understand the goals, dynamics, challenges, and politics, we can navigate these more effectively.

3. *Perception awareness*: What perceptions do you have of others and what assumptions are you making based on those perceptions? What assumptions are you making about yourself based on your perceptions? On the other side, what perceptions do people have of you? If you were to ask your friends, colleagues, direct reports, and so on what they think of you, and if they were to answer honestly, would you like their answer? When I deliver 360-degree feedback to my clients, one of the biggest joys is when they finally realize that their colleagues hold them in much higher regard than they thought. This not only validates their leadership style, but it also gives them permission to be bolder, to embrace their influencing power and use it.

---

[32] Jack Zenger and Joseph Folkman, "We Like Leaders Who Underrate Themselves," *Harvard Business Review,* November 10, 2015, https://hbr.org/2015/11/we-like-leaders-who-underrate-themselves.

On the other hand, if the feedback isn't positive, the person now has data points regarding the impact of their behavior and, with the help of a coach, an action plan to address the issue. In both cases, whether the responses are positive or negative, the person can turn the information into constructive feedback.

The more aware you are about yourself, the social arena in which you work, and the perceptions of others, the more likely you are to make strategic decisions about people and the relationships you build.

In the past, people prioritized individual drivers of success: passion, hard work, talent, knowledge, and luck. In today's complex and highly interconnected world, however, success is also increasingly dependent on how we interact with others. In his book *Give and Take*, Adam Grant categorizes people into three buckets: givers, takers, and matchers. Givers are always giving, sometimes to their own detriment. Takers interact with people when they need something. Matchers interact on a quid pro quo basis: "Sure, I'll do this for you, but you'll give me something in return."

Grant's model is helpful in terms of developing self-awareness—are you a giver, taker, or matcher? It's also useful in thinking about the people you form relationships with. From a purely selfish, resilience-building perspective, it's advantageous to associate with as many givers as possible and become a true giver. In his book, Grant shows evidence that in the marathon that is life, givers tend to become more successful and fulfilled than matchers and takers.

In the Interpersonal Dynamics (a.k.a. Touchy-Feely) class I facilitate at Stanford University Graduate School of Business, we have a saying: you are not evaluated by your intentions but by your impact. As leaders, we are always creating impact, so the question is what sort of impact do you want to have?

Still, it's important to realize that intention doesn't automatically translate into the desired impact. Missing this truth is a common issue among those I coach. Julio, for example, is the young CFO of a very successful global technology company. He loves the organization, its product, and the impact it has on the world. As one of the first employees of the company, he also has a sense of responsibility that drives him to do more than required and he has a high bar for himself and others.

When I first met Julio, his level of engagement and commitment to the company's success was evident. Yet other members of the executive team perceived him as a controlling, micromanaging workaholic, as well as a competitive individual. It was not Julio's intention to be any of those things, yet his actions were perceived as such. His intention was to do a good job, to help the company and his team grow, but the impact on others didn't align with his intent.

In the Interpersonal Dynamics class at Stanford, students regularly give each other feedback. For example, one student raised his hand every time he wanted to speak. After several class sessions, other students noticed his behavior and started making assumptions about him. One person asked him, "Why do you raise your hand all the time? You remind me of a kid trying to ask permission to go to the bathroom. I think that reduces the level of influence you have with me."

Someone else chimed in and said, "Wait, that's not how I see it. I see it as a lack of respect because when he raises his hand, it's like he's cutting to the front of the line. On a couple of occasions there were other people who wanted to speak, but by raising his hand, he's saying, 'No, wait, I'm going now. Listen to what I have to say.'"

Two different perceptions and two different assumptions about the same action created impacts that the student never intended.

If you find yourself saying "That is not what I meant," the impact of your behavior probably does not align with your intention. In most cases, unfortunately, we don't even know what the impact is; we only see the result of the impact (e.g., defensiveness, resistance, a communication gap), which will most likely lead to us making assumptions about the other person that aren't true.

> **INTENTIONAL RELATIONSHIP-BUILDING QUESTIONS**
>
> - What assumptions are you making about yourself?
> - What assumptions are you making about others?
> - How do you want to use this relationship?
> - How does this relationship add to what you need to accomplish?
> - What do you need help with?
> - Who can help you with this problem?
> - What characteristics are you looking for?
> - What stories are you making up about yourself or others that might prevent you from taking advantage of this particular relationship? (e.g., are you thinking you're not good enough, or that they aren't?)

ENGAGE PEOPLE

Have you ever heard someone say, "I am a self-made man/woman"? That comment implies the person reached their current position or success without help, but that couldn't be further from the truth. We all need people to progress in life, whether personally or professionally. That self-made mindset is also dangerous because it discourages cooperation; collaboration and cooperation beat competition and individual effort anytime. Shared labor always outmatches the efforts of an isolated genius.

Smart individuals don't bask in personal glorification. They know that they are standing where they are because of the collaboration and contribution of many other individuals who helped them get to the top: parents, spouses, teachers, coaches, mentors, partners, and even competitors.

When you consider adding a mentor or other relationship, you have to be clear about what you need, how the person can help, and, most importantly, what impact you want to have on those you engage. You also need to be intentional in the way you build those relationships.

HOW TO ENGAGE

When I describe the five key relationships framework to my clients, many respond with "Oh, yeah, I need to network." When we network, however, we focus on what we get from others. It is self-serving, and sometimes that intention is obvious to the individual we want to engage. When we build relationships and form alliances, however, we focus on what we can give and provide, as well as what we can get. That mindset allows us to see people differently—as people we want to help and support, not simply take from. Seeing people differently allows us to think differently, which allows us to show up differently.

Building relationships goes deeper than networking, and it starts with being a giver. The law of reciprocity comes into play here: for every action there is a reaction. If you are a giver, people will give back to you. As Adam Grant put it in his book

Give and Take, "This is what I find most magnetic about successful givers: they get to the top without cutting others down, finding ways of expanding the pie that benefit themselves and the people around them. Whereas success is zero-sum in a group of takers, in groups of givers, it may be true that the whole is greater than the sum of the parts."[33]

RULES OF INFLUENCE

One Sunday, I waited for a spot in the grocery store parking lot. I saw a car leaving on the other side, so I drove around to take it. When I got there, I realized that the lady who had been behind me had cut through the space between two handicapped spaces and was now trying to move into the newly opened spot. The problem was that she needed to back up in order to angle her car into the space, and my car was in the way. I tried to signal that the spot was mine, but she wasn't having it. Through the windshield, I could see her screaming and waving her arms, obviously getting ready for a confrontation.

Finally, I got out of my car and approached the woman. "I'm sorry if I'm being rude," I said. "I just wanted to let you know that I was here before you. You saw me over there in line. So, I believe this spot should be mine. But I see that you're in a hurry, so you're welcome to have it. Let me back up."

"You weren't being rude," the woman said, visibly disarmed by my words.

"Okay, great. Then let me just back up since you're in a bigger hurry than I am."

"No, no. I'm sorry. Let me back up. It's yours."

---

[33] Adam Grant, *Give and Take: Why Helping Others Drives Our Success* (New York: Penguin Books, 2013), 560 (e-book).

This would not have been the conclusion if I had met the woman's screaming with my own. I treated her with kindness, and she decided to do the same. I created the momentum I wanted her to follow, rather than following the momentum she created by being upset. When we saw each other inside the grocery store, she smiled at me. That smile was a bigger reward than the parking spot.

Humans are in the business of selling. We sell a product, ourselves, our friendship, our ideas, our needs. To successfully sell anything, we need a certain level of influence. Sometimes, we get in our own way when it comes to exerting influence like this, as my client Jack learned.

Jack was having a hard time getting things done through others. After he started following the five rules of influence that follow, he had an aha moment: focusing on results and focusing on relationships are not mutually exclusive. "When a leader starts with relationships, a team can accomplish a lot," he told me. "I have been managing people for a long time. I cannot believe I am learning about this now." Jack made some personal changes in the way he interacted with his direct reports. If he hadn't made those changes, he probably could have produced the same results, but by adapting, he has increased his influence with his direct reports and made life easier for himself at the same time.

Here are the five rules that can significantly increase your influence with others.

Rule 1: Be Open to Being Influenced

If we want to influence and move people, we first need to be open to being influenced. We need to remember that we don't know everything about everything. If we approach conversations and relationships with a closed mind, we lose influence.

People at all levels want to know that they are relevant, and one way to communicate this is being open to hear and learn from people, even if their perspectives and opinions are different from your own. Many clients have told me that they are more open to express their opinion if they can tell the other person cares about what they have to say. That kind of person is open to being influenced.

My client April, a recently hired team leader for a biotech startup, came from a much better-established organization where many processes and roles were well-defined. She was struggling to get buy-in from her peers and collaborators, and at the core of their resistance was the perception that April was somewhat closed-minded and inflexible.

April started communicating to others that she was interested in hearing what they had to say. By asking clarifying questions like "What do you think of this approach?" and "Is there another way to do this?" she encouraged others to propose solutions. She communicated that her opinion was an option, not the final position on the matter. By improving her listening skills and letting go of the idea that her way was the only way, April sent a signal to others that she was open to being influenced.

Rule 2: Be Trustworthy

Many people live by the mentality that trust needs to be earned. Again, following the law of reciprocity that for every action there's a reaction, I think the opposite is true: we should extend trust first. If people perceive that you trust them, your level of influence will go up.

At the same time, we should make sure we are people worth trusting. According to Stephen Covey, our trustworthiness is based on a combination of competencies (skills, knowledge, experience, credibility, performance, and our record) and character traits (caring, transparency, openness, honesty, fairness, authenticity).[34] If we focus on building both sides of the matrix, competence and character, we will be perceived as trustworthy, which will cause people to trust us, which will gain us influence. If we have the competencies to help people and every intention to do them good, then we are extending trust in both ways: we are trusting this person, and we are showing that we are worthy of being trusted.

There is a correlation between personal connection and the level of influence: the greater the connection, the greater the influence. As leaders, we need to connect first, then lead. If two people connect at a personal level, they will most likely be open to each other's influence. Whether with cross-functional peers, direct reports, or superiors, you need to connect and build trust before others will deem you a competent leader worthy of trust.

Take Sheryl, a newly appointed manager to a financial group. She inherited an unengaged team that didn't trust their previous leader. Her first order of business was to connect with each team member. One individual told Sheryl that he hadn't taken all his vacation days in over two years. Sheryl told him, "My commitment to you is to make sure you can take this vacation within the next two months." She made similar commitments to each team member, promising to take care of issues that were in the realm of her possibilities. By showing

---

[34] Stephen M. R. Covey, *The Speed of Trust* (London: Simon and Schuster, 2008).

her personal intentions toward her team, she immediately built trust.

To build trust and thus influence, you must get to know the people you are leading and establish strong working relationships with them. Start by setting up one-on-one meetings with all key team members to help you understand their motivations, points of view, aspirations, and goals. Also, come ready with your project elevator pitch. Like a personal elevator pitch, this is a succinct vision of your plans for the future. What does success look like for the project, team, or initiative you are leading? This is critical as you need to enroll others into your vision of the future. Before ending the conversation, be sure to ask, "Do you have what you need to achieve your goals? How can I help you get there?"

They need to know that you are looking out for them, respect their contribution, and will recognize them for a job well done. With this shift, their level of trust increases, and so does your influence as a leader.

Rule 3: Communicate with Empathy and Vulnerability

In my effort to become a giver, I got involved in a program that helps other coaches hone their skills and facilitated a group of highly successful coaches. During the first meeting, we needed time for personal introductions. Usually, each person often highlights various accomplishments, positions, degrees, and so forth. Being in some of those groups myself, I noticed that rather than increasing influence, this kind of bragging session can create separation and competition.

I wanted to create an environment of collaboration and psychological safety, not competition, so I took a different approach. When we had our first meeting and time for introductions came, I asked each person to share the answer to two questions: (1) where they grew up and (2) the biggest challenge they had growing up.

Something magical happened in that first session. People started self-disclosing the challenges and pain they experienced as children. They started to reveal their humanity. Pain and suffering are universal, and the experience of vulnerability, sharing, and listening connected this group tremendously.

Being empathetic and vulnerable strengthens your level of influence because you are perceived as more approachable. In an interview with the *New York Times*, Peter Löscher, former president and CEO of Siemens AG, remarked, "I'm always telling people, 'Look, I make a mistake every day.'"[35] This level of vulnerability encouraged his employees to openly admit that they, too, make mistakes.

Leading with empathy and vulnerability also encourages compassion for one's self and others. After admitting he makes a mistake every day, Löscher said, "but hopefully I am not making the same mistake twice." Self-compassion is about giving ourselves permission to not be perfect, and to also look for improvement. When people see that combination in a leader, their trust increases and they are encouraged to do the same.

Rule 4: Sweat the Small Stuff

One of my coaching clients recently broke the trust he had with one of his coworkers. In his mind it was no big deal and his coworker needed to deal with it and move on.

---

35 Adam Bryant, "The Trust That Makes a Team Click," *New York Times*, July 31, 2011, https://www.nytimes.com/2011/07/31/business/siemens-ceo-on-building-trust-and-teamwork.html.

"What would happen if I did to you what you did to your coworker?" I asked during one meeting. "What would you expect me to do?"

"I would expect you to apologize," he said.

"Do you see the irony?"

"I absolutely see it, but it's not a big deal!"

I tried to show him that even though it wasn't a big deal to him, it was to his coworker.

When you want to be influential, you have to keep in mind that just because something isn't a big deal or important to you doesn't mean it isn't for someone else. Telling someone "Get over it," "Don't worry about it," or "What are you afraid of?" is not helpful.

My client Jack, mentioned earlier in the influence section, is a natural risk taker. He attended Harvard followed by business school and then started working for a consulting company. His whole life has been shaped by taking risks. Now he works for a grocery store chain and he has been identified as high potential. He is doing a rotation in different areas of the organization, and part of his current job is to design training protocols for the operators—the managers, owners, and people at every level who work at the stores.

Jack had a chance to promote one of the managers in his organization. He felt it was a great opportunity for this individual and he was excited to do it. But when he offered the promotion, the worker turned it down. Jack was stunned. He couldn't understand why somebody would pass up on a growth opportunity like that, so he asked. "It's too risky" was the manager's response. This was an individual who had grown in the company and was very happy, satisfied, and engaged where he was. If he were promoted and did not succeed in his new job, he would probably have to leave the company. Even though there was a financial incentive, he felt safe where he was and couldn't put his family at risk.

I encouraged Jack to acknowledge the manager's concern, that it would be a risk, and then coach him through it so he felt secure about taking the step. For Jack, taking that step wasn't a big deal, but it was huge for this manager. That's the small stuff we need to sweat. What might be comfortable or less risky or no big deal to us might be completely different for someone else. We earn influence by acknowledging the needs, concerns, values, and perspectives of the other person.

Rule 5: Add Value

As mentioned, in his book *Give and Take*, Adam Grant makes a compelling case for givers—people who are always adding value to others. In their personal and professional lives, givers cultivate a reputation of altruism, collaboration, and hard work, which wins the respect and admiration not only of those to whom they give, but also of observers.

When you mentor someone, for example, you are adding value to that person's life and work. That's incredibly powerful. An unintended consequence is that others—your manager, perhaps—will see you as someone who invests in others and transfers knowledge, which are important leadership skills.

According to Grant, being a giver can also unlock your own success and your capacity to find purpose at work. Contributing to the lives of others, believing in them and their goals and aspirations, is a sure way to gain their support, which in turn strengthens your social resilience.

TAKE CARE OF YOUR RELATIONSHIPS

Building relationships might be the most underappreciated pillar. We interact with people every day and assume that connections will magically appear, so we often fail to form alliances with intentionality.

Our Western culture tends to promote execution at the speed of light, focusing on results and short-term gains, at a big unintended cost. For example, the first order of business when starting a new role is often to show your capabilities by securing a quick win early. You want to prove yourself, deliver results, and show management they made the right choice in you.

However, many times this relentless pursuit of the quick win is focused on results and not on the people you work with. This approach will have some negative consequences on you and your relationships, often leading to burned bridges, overworked teams, and poor morale.

This lack of focus on building relationships diminishes your ability to influence, and this is a critical mistake. As author Stephen Covey points out, "You simply can't think about efficiency with people. You think about effectiveness with people and efficiency with things."[36]

Economists and consultants love to talk about ROI (return on investment), but according to Tommy Spaulding, author of *It's Not Just Who You Know*, we should be equally concerned with ROR (return on relationships). Return on relationships is the value you gain from nurturing authentic relationships with your connections, clients, colleagues, and community with zero expectations. Doing so leads to long-term gains in the form of trust, friendship, and, ultimately, social resilience.

---

[36] Covey, *7 Habits of Highly Successful People*, 351 (e-book).

It's impossible to build a successful career or organization in a silo. We need others to get through our professional life, as well as personal, and this involves social resilience.

As is probably clear by now, building resilience is an endless journey, and you already have what you need to get started. Don't discount the relationships you already have. Start there and then figure out what kind of relationships you want to add and intentionally start building them. The longer you have these relationships, the stronger they will become and the more useful they will be in terms of building resilience, both yours and theirs.

On to the fifth pillar—it's time to Find Your Inner Strength.

RECAP: BUILD RELATIONSHIPS

Relationships are critical to our social and overall resilience. We need to consciously and intentionally create connections and form alliances before we need them.

Identify Relationships

Bring into your life people who add value, bring positive energy, and have different perspectives.

We all need at least one mentor, sponsor, partner, mentee, and competitor in our lives. Which relationship are you currently lacking?

Evaluate Perceptions

One of the most courageous things we can do is see ourselves as others see us. The other is to evaluate our perceptions of others.

What assumptions have you made about yourself and others? How might these be getting in the way of forming meaningful and rewarding relationships?

Engage People

The best way to engage people is to nurture authentic relationships with zero expectations.

Are you a giver, an amplifier, and a person of value in those relationships?

Chapter 7

FIND YOUR INNER STRENGTH

Your strength isn't measured by your doubts but by the boundless courage that emerges when you challenge your own limits.

- *Raise* your standards, set higher goals, and expand your comfort zone.
- *Understand* your choices between risk and safety.
- *Take action* by using empowering rituals, habits, grit, and focus.

In July 2012, I was in the best shape of my life. I had finished the Western States 100 a couple months earlier. I felt healthy. I was happily remarried. I loved my job. I was traveling to Guatemala often to see my parents. Life was good.

Then it came time for my annual MRI, and I had the scan and subsequent appointment with a new neurosurgeon.

When the doctor walked in and saw me sitting there, he asked, "Where is the patient?"

"I'm the patient," I said.

"No, that's impossible. With your MRI, I was expecting to see someone with visible neurological problems. What have you been doing?"

"Uh, I have been running," I said and then told him about my recent adventure of finishing the Western States 100.

"Well, it seems that has paid off, because you have adapted to this tumor. Obviously, you have no visible symptoms, but you have a ticking time bomb in your head and we need to take care of it right away."

Oh God, I thought. *Not again.* It had been nine years since my first brain surgery. I had always known a second surgery was a possibility, but the news still hit me hard. Now I knew what the recovery process was like, and naturally, I worried about the possible impact on my marriage and new job.

When I told my boss about it, he was very supportive and told me to take as much time as I needed to get better. Two weeks before my surgery, however, he called me into his office to let me know that the company was experiencing financial issues and they had decided to let me go.

I weighed my options and considered hiring a lawyer, as I thought the company's actions were illegal, not to mention unkind. My wife encouraged me to let it go for now and focus on the surgery.

Despite my concerns, my recovery from the second surgery was nothing like the first. Within eight weeks, I was pretty much back to normal, and I credit my speedy recovery to the fact that I had been in resilience training. Over the years, I had adopted keystone habits that benefitted every aspect of my being. I had developed physical resilience through running, swimming, cycling, and eating right. I had developed mental resilience through learning. I had developed spiritual resilience by cultivating gratefulness and looking for the three gifts in any situation. But most importantly, I had adopted the practice of *amor fati*. I knew I could not change the outcome of my surgery or the length of my recovery, so I chose to love my fate, no matter what it was.

This story illustrates one of my main goals in writing this book: although I do want to help you adapt and thrive if you're currently in a crisis, even more, I want to show you the importance of intentionally exercising that resilience muscle every day so it's there when you need it.

Inner strength is a key part of your ability to accept a harsh reality and motivate yourself to move forward. In this chapter, we'll consider how you find your inner strength by raising your standards, understanding your choices, and taking action through empowering rituals.

RAISE YOUR STANDARDS

You've probably heard the saying that you don't know how strong you are until you have no choice. I'll add that when you think you cannot go any farther, you can. The fact is, we're all stronger than we think we are, and we have to raise the expectations we have for ourselves.

In Chinese culture, children born in the year of the dragon are believed to be destined for greatness. They are considered special, more intelligent, and sure to go far in life. As a result, the number of marriages goes up prior to a dragon year, and births increase considerably.

In 2017, Professors Naci H. Mocan and Han Yu researched this year-of-the-dragon phenomenon and determined that kids born in the year of the dragon do indeed go to school earlier, learn faster, and get farther in life. However, it isn't because these children are more intelligent. Because parents have higher expectations of children born in the year of the dragon, those kids rise to the occasion.[37]

Similarly, Alfred Oberlander, the manager of a New York insurance company, observed that new insurance agents performed better in outstanding agencies than in average or poor agencies. So, he assigned his best agents to work with his best manager in a top agency. As expected, this group produced 40 percent of the total sales of the agency.[38]

Like children born in the year of the dragon, these agents saw themselves as special because of what was communicated, and they worked to meet those expectations.

Today, companies spend a lot of resources identifying high potentials. Then they reinforce the idea that they will do well, they've got what it takes, they'll take over for the CEO one day—and they do. Often these assertions are based on expectations, not identifiable qualities, but those expectations cause people to think of themselves differently, seek better results, and perform at a higher level.

In all three cases, raised standards result in individuals rising to meet those expectations. This is a key component of resiliency. Having a moonshot goal—a high, lofty target to shoot for—motivates us to take risks, make mistakes, get up, and try again, with the end result being increased resilience and higher performance.

---

[37] Naci H. Mocan and Han Yu, "Can Superstition Create a Self-Fulfilling Prophecy? School Outcomes of Dragon Children of China," National Bureau of Economic Research, August 2017, https://www.nber.org/papers/w23709.

[38] J. Sterling Livingston, "Pygmalion in Management," *Harvard Business Review* (January 2003), https://hbr.org/2003/01/pygmalion-in-management.

This particular phenomenon was first studied by Robert Rosenthal and Leone Jacobson.[39] They told teachers that based on the results of a "sophisticated test," certain students could be expected to be high performers in the classroom. In reality, there was no test and the high performers were randomly chosen.

Rosenthal and Jacobson made two key observations: (1) teachers spent more time with the high performers and (2) the high performers responded positively to this attention and to the expectation that they were different and perhaps superior. In other words, the expectations placed on the children affected how they responded. Rosenthal and Jacobson referred to these results as the Pygmalion Effect, or self-fulfilling prophecy. In essence, our actions toward others impact others' beliefs about us, which in turn cause others' actions toward us, which then reinforce our beliefs about ourselves, which then influence our actions toward others—only to start the cycle all over again.

The connection between the Pygmalion Effect and the ability to adapt and thrive has also been studied in Israeli teachers. The author concluded that the Pygmalion Effect indeed contributed to building resilience.[40]

The term *moonshot* was born after President John F. Kennedy set a lofty goal of landing a man on the moon and bringing him safely back to Earth. It came to represent any "difficult

---

39 Robert Rosenthal and Lenore Jacobson, "Pygmalion in the Classroom," *Urban Review* 3 (1968): 16–20.

40 Mary Gutman, "Retrospective View of the Early Career: Three Landmarks in Building Resilience in Academic Administration among Israeli Teacher Training College Principals," *Journal of Educational Administration and History* 52, no. 2: 165–77.

or expensive task, the outcome of which is expected to have great significance."[41]

Since the moon landing in 1969, amazing inventions and discoveries have resulted from moonshot goals. In 2010, Google founders Larry Page and Sergey Brin formed a new arm of the company to work on moonshots: far-out, sci-fi technologies that one day will make a difference in the world. The company is called X, or the moonshot factory, which deals solely with these impossible goals.

To embrace this mindset, ask yourself: "What is one outrageous thing I can do to solve this problem or to add more value?" When we have that moonshot mentality, we start exploring bigger options and opportunities, which is a fundamental part of adapting and thriving.

Pursuing big goals is scary. It involves taking risks, making mistakes, and learning on the way forward. Raising your standards involves becoming comfortable with being uncomfortable. It means pushing yourself to expand your comfort zone a little at a time.

A moonshot doesn't happen all at once. If someone wants to run a marathon, they can't simply put on a pair of shoes and run 26.2 miles. That's a sure way to get injured. Instead, they might increase mileage a little at a time, even just 10 percent on each run. Then try running a little faster. Then longer, then faster, and so on. I didn't think I would be able to run a marathon, but I did. I didn't think I would be able to complete an Ironman triathlon, but I did. In both cases, I increased my strength and capacity a little at a time. We are all more capable than we think we are.

---

[41] Scott D. Anthony and Mark Johnson, "What a Good Moonshot is Really For," *Harvard Business Review*, May 14, 2013, https://hbr.org/2013/05/what-a-good-moonshot-is-really-2.

How do you get closer to your moonshot goal? Here are four simple steps that have worked for me:

- *Step 1: Shoot for the moon.* Set an aspirational goal. For me, writing this book was an aspirational goal.
- *Step 2: Develop a strategy.* Create a plan for reaching that goal. I decided to hire Scribe Media to help me write and edit this book.
- *Step 3: Set smaller goals to measure progress.* Take the big pieces of your strategy and break them into smaller steps to put the strategy into action. My editor and I scheduled phone calls, broke down the book idea into chapters, and talked through all of the content to bring this book to life.
- *Step 4: Adopt winning rituals.* Habits and rituals allow you to execute the smaller goals and overall strategy. I started getting up at five o'clock every morning to write and to prepare for my calls with my editor.

My client Tyrell reached a certain level in his organization and then the promotions stopped. He considered leaving the company because he didn't see the point of staying if he had gone as far as he could go. He came into the company aiming to become the CFO, he was told he was going to become the CFO, yet after two years the CFO role remained open.

One day I asked, "What do you want?"

"You mean here?" Tyrell asked, a little confused.

"Anywhere really. What do you want to be in, say, five years, whether in this company or somewhere else? What do you really want to be?"

Without hesitation, Tyrell said, "I want to be CFO, but the company—"

I interrupted him and said, "What if you take the company

out of the equation and set a moonshot goal of being CFO, period?"

"Yeah, but my company—"

"Forget your company. If your goal is to be CFO, whether at this company or somewhere else, what skills do you need to acquire? What disruptions do you have to make to get yourself ready for that CFO role, no matter where it happens?"

After thinking for a minute, Tyrell said, "First, I need to know more about how to think like a CFO." In that statement, he had a strategy (Step 2) to attain his moonshot goal of becoming CFO (Step 1).

As a result of that conversation, Tyrell enrolled in a couple of classes for CFOs and set up interviews with other CFOs in his network (Step 3: set smaller goals). Finally, he knew that unless he carved some time to act on what he had learned, everything would stay in the "I wish I had more time" list. So, he started setting aside a certain number of hours a week specifically to work on reaching his goal (Step 4: adopt winning rituals).

Shortly before this book went to print, Tyrell left his company to become CFO of a large retail chain. He told me that his mindset shift was instrumental in seeing himself as someone who could make that move.

We often tie our personal growth to a company rather than who we want to become. If you focus on the job, rather than being, you limit yourself. Instead, focus on the process of becoming the kind of person who could hold that role. Let your aspirational goal stretch you as a person, not as a title.

If you have a higher standard, you will see yourself differently. You will attempt the difficult tasks, go through the pain, and endure discomfort to fulfill the view you have of yourself. Here again the drivers of resilience are in play: *optimism* allows you to shoot for the moon, *commitment* pushes you to create a strategy, and *persistence* gives you the grit to move forward in the face of discomfort.

Disruptions, moonshot goals, getting comfortable with discomfort, raising your standards—these are all important ways to exercise and build your resilience muscle and find inner strength. Tyrell already had everything he needed to take the first step, and that first step is how anyone pursues an audacious moonshot goal.

There is no growth in comfort. We need to embrace living outside our comfort zone—or expanding that zone a little at a time. When your road is veiled in mystery, you have the chance to blaze your own trail, painting the story of your journey with every step.

UNDERSTAND YOUR CHOICES

Widely attributed to psychologist Abraham Maslow, "life is an ongoing process of choosing between safety and risk." Sometimes we choose safety out of a defensive posture, sometimes we do so to maintain the status quo, and sometimes we simply want to be sheltered and avoid risk. When we choose risk, we know it might be uncomfortable, but we do it anyway for the sake of progress and growth. Either way, whether we choose safety or risk, we're making a choice.

We always have a choice. Period. If you start from that truth, it's easier to be empowered to make a choice, even in situations where you think you don't have one. Resilience involves the ability to exercise that choice, even when the options seem equally hard or unpleasant. When we know that we have a choice, we can exercise a sense of control, a need that is innate in all of us.

Let's consider some categories of choices we have.

GRAVITY VERSUS SITUATIONAL PROBLEMS

As mentioned earlier, solving for gravity problems can lead to unnecessary stress and frustration, for they are impossible to solve. The key is to see the real problem in each challenge—the situational problem we can actually solve—and choose to take the first step toward solving it.

In my second meeting with Angelica, I asked, "What's important for you today? What is something you're dealing with right now?"

"My boss is a difficult person to understand," she said. "First, I was asked to develop my direct reports, so I started bringing my direct reports to meetings so they could give the presentation. I also started delegating more. Apparently, my boss doesn't think either of those choices is a good idea."

As Angelica saw it, the problem to solve was getting her boss to see that she was trying to figure out how to manage her people, and bringing them along to practice presenting seemed like a chance to develop them. In her mind, that act should have shown her boss that she was doing something about the feedback he gave her.

Angelica told me more about the conversations she had with her boss after one of the meetings where her directs gave the presentation, and I caught a glimpse of the true problem. It wasn't what her direct reports did or even the questions her boss asked. The issue was that both Angelica and her boss were somewhat surprised. The boss was surprised that the direct reports showed up and gave the presentation, and Angelica was surprised that her boss thought this was a problem.

Angelica was trying to make her boss see things differently, but that wasn't her problem to solve. Her problem was to develop her direct reports and to do so in a way that aligned with her manager's expectations. She could not control his response. What she could control was her actions: what she could do to diminish the element of surprise by drafting a simple action plan for developing her direct reports and then sharing that with her manager.

As Maslow said, life is an ongoing process of choosing between safety and risk. For Angelica, the risk was seeing the problem as something completely different than what she was thinking. In some ways it was safer to stick with the known outcome—an upset boss—because that was familiar and, thus, comfortable in some way.

If you understand the problems that are yours to solve and those that aren't, you can make choices that will actually move you forward.

SHOULD VERSUS MUST VERSUS COULD

Understanding your choices also involves understanding the difference between *should*, *must*, and *could*. When we say, "Oh, I should do that," chances are, we won't. *Should* and *could* indicate wishful thinking. The shoulds are probably important, but not urgent. The coulds are usually the easiest tasks that will produce a busy feeling that sometimes we mistake for productivity. But the fact remains that these are not action-driven words. *Must*, on the other hand, is. When we say, "I must do that," chances are much higher that we actually will. The must dos are the top priorities that must be done, the critical work that directly contributes to your goal achievement.

The difference between these three words is powerful. *Should* means you have some degree of obligation or best interest. It is usually something you can do, but isn't a necessity: I should wash my hands before dinner.

Could means that you have the ability to do it, but the benefits or the obligations are not there. It implies a possibility: I could wash my hands before dinner.

Using *must* denotes an obligation, an unavoidable necessity, and it usually is followed by action: I must wash my hands (or risk getting sick).

Take note of how you talk to yourself. Do you say *should* or *must* when you're thinking about a new action, a new step? Resilience involves action, taking the first step forward toward change. Using words that compel us to move is one way to get started. Telling yourself "I must do X" makes the action non-negotiable. In saying "I must," you commit to do something.

My wife is a physician, and she declares to herself every day, "I must be home by 7:30, or I'll miss dinner with the family." This is a way to declare to herself a non-negotiable task that must be done.

MARATHON VERSUS SPRINT

In life there are marathons and there are sprints. If we live like everything is a sprint, we will burn out rather quickly because sprinting is unsustainable for long distances.

A while ago, someone asked me, "What must I do to finish an ultramarathon?" After thinking about it, I told him there are three musts: setting your pace, maintaining your nutrition, and taking care of your feet. Sometimes, ignoring any one of those could mean not finishing the race. All too often, runners go out too fast at the start of a race, using up all the energy they will need to get them to the finish line. Many runners also forget to fuel and drink correctly—they forget to put the right fuel in the tank and at the right times. And runners often fail to take care of their feet, which is paramount at ultra distances. Even a small pebble can create a nasty and painful blister. It can easily cause a runner to change their stride, which then causes pain in the hip or knee, which could lead to dropping out.

The first two times I ran the Javelina 100 in Arizona, I broke rule number one—don't go out too fast. The course is fairly flat with few hills to force me to slow down, so without realizing it I went out too fast on the first two twenty-mile loops, and I couldn't sustain the pace. At the end of the third loop, I had to abandon the race.

It's possible to go out too fast in your career, too. I have coached leaders who want to get to the finish line as fast as they can—young leaders who expect to be promoted right away and entrepreneurs who want to get their product to market as soon as possible. We have to remember that our careers are a marathon, not a sprint, and sometimes to go far, we must slow down. We have to deliberately choose our pacing, assess the path to get to the next level, and take the steps one at a time to get there, making sure we take in proper "nutrition" (reading, skill building, relationship building) and "take care of our feet" (maximize the resources we currently have).

Like our careers, life itself is like a marathon. It is long and includes sprints, where we move as fast as we can for a short distance, but in the long run, that speed is unsustainable. Understanding when life's a sprint and when it's a marathon will allow you to make decisions about pacing, nutrition, and caring for your feet.

SPEED VERSUS VELOCITY

Speed and velocity are distinct concepts. Speed refers to the rate of motion, calculated as the distance traveled divided by the time taken. However, it's worth noting that one can move quickly without necessarily changing position significantly. For example, when running in circles or following a path that leads back to your starting point, your speed may be high because you're covering a lot of distance in a short time. However, your displacement (change in position) remains relatively small because you end up back where you began. In contrast, velocity not only accounts for speed but also takes into consideration the direction and displacement of an object from its starting point.

Many leaders focus on the incredible number of things they need to do. They move quickly in a lot of directions doing a lot of things, so they think they're being productive. This couldn't be further from the truth. To be truly productive and move closer to our goals, we need to focus on velocity, not speed.

One day in our coaching session, my client Michelle told me about a volunteer opportunity at work that involved designing the internal space in their new office. "I jumped at the opportunity because I think this is a great chance to do something different, something more visible."

A couple weeks later, Michelle gave me an update. "There is so much work to do. I have to X and Y. It's a lot."

"Michelle," I said, "remind me—why did you choose to do this?"

"I want to show that I can help and add value."

"It seems like you're doing a lot more work. Do you think these tasks make you more promotable?"

Michelle had to admit they did not. She had taken on this work as a way to reach her goal of being promoted faster. In truth, however, that work did not increase the skills she needed to be promoted, so it actually decreased the velocity at which she moved toward her goal.

So, how do we choose velocity over speed so that our actions do effectively move us forward?

First, manage your attention, not your time. There are just twenty-four hours in a day, which means you have a finite amount of time in which to do what needs to be done. If you continue piling on tasks, you will run out of time. Instead, keep your goal in mind and prioritize your activities in terms of what pushes you toward that goal. Think about what needs your attention, and then fill your time based on those priorities.

Second, be ruthless about saying no to the unnecessary tasks, meetings, and "special projects" that come your way. Saying yes to requests from bosses, teammates, and others can make us feel essential and important, but this is a sure recipe for burnout and could decrease our velocity and thus prove detrimental to our long-term goal.

Saying no to your boss, however, might be tricky, so you need to find ways to do so that don't come across as unengaged, negative, or even lazy. In this case, don't rely on your willpower to say no, but rather create a system that allows you to consistently say no with grace and clarity.

One of my favorite strategies is to say yes, but very slowly. When your manager asks you to do something that you don't think is "promotable work," simply say, "I think I can do that and make it a priority. Which one of these projects do I need to de-prioritize?" Or "In order for me to do this, I need X resource. How do you suggest I go about getting that?"

The commitment driver of resilience plays a role here. When you are committed to a goal or project, you allow yourself to prioritize ruthlessly in pursuit of that goal.

EFFICIENCY VERSUS EFFECTIVENESS

People use these two terms interchangeably, but they are actually very different. *Efficiency* describes a process—how something is done. *Effectiveness* describes a person's interaction with that process—how well they use it. As stated in Chapter 6, "effectiveness with people and efficiency with things," according to Stephen Covey.[42]

For example, washing clothes in a washing machine is an efficient process. Step 1: put the clothes in the washer. Step 2: put the soap in the machine. Step 3: turn on the machine. When the machine stops, the clothes are clean. Done.

However, if the person washing clothes forgets to put in soap or throws a red sock in with the white load of laundry, the innately efficient process will not be effective; either the clothes will not be clean and the load will have to be rewashed, or the load will be pink and the person will need to buy new clothes. As discussed in Chapter 6, when people join a new company or are promoted, they often want to hit the ground running, so they focus on securing a quick win to showcase their capabilities and show their efficiency. Unfortunately, in this relentless pursuit of the quick win, people often focus on the outcome and not the people they need to help them secure those wins, now and in the future. This shortsightedness can lead to burned bridges and overworked teams, both of which can compromise your effectiveness at getting things done in the future.

In the end, we are all in the business of building trust and moving people one way or the other. Focusing on people and establishing strong relationships with them will increase your effectiveness and enable you to maximize the efficiency of your task at hand.

---

42 Covey, *7 Habits of Highly Successful People*, 351 (e-book).

PRACTICE VERSUS DELIBERATE PRACTICE

The choice here is simple: we can mindlessly work our craft again and again, hoping to improve, or we can train and practice in a purposeful and systematic way that guarantees improvement.

When I competed in my second Ironman, I swam over 250,000 yards over the course of a year to prepare for the swim part of the event. I applied the same concept to my running and biking: I ran and biked a lot of miles, thinking volume was a recipe for getting better. After all of this work, I expected to do well, but I arrived at the race overtrained and tired, and I did not perform as hoped. This is a very common mistake among athletes known as overtraining syndrome, which happens when they don't adequately recover after repetitive intense training.[43]

In Chapter 4, I mentioned that I trained differently for my third Ironman, specifically the swim part of the race. Instead of focusing on the volume of swimming, I worked on my swim efficiency. In addition, I focused on increasing my overall strength using CrossFit, high-intensity exercise that emphasizes load, distance, and speed on the whole body. That combination—focusing on my swimming form and getting stronger—was a great recipe. With only one quarter of the swimming volume I had done in preparation for my second Ironman, in my third race I clocked my fastest time to date.

Benjamin Bloom, a professor at the University of Chicago, looked into 120 elite performers in various domains, from music to math to neurology. In addition to finding no correlation between IQ and performance, he learned that the amount

---

43 Jeffrey B. Kreher and Jennifer B. Schwartz, "Overtraining Syndrome," *Sports Health* 4, no. 2 (2012): 128–38, https://www.ncbi.nlm.nih.gov/pmc/articles/PMC3435910/.

and, more importantly, the quality of practice were key factors in the level of expertise people achieved.[44]

How does this translate into leadership? As in any sport, deliberate practice in leadership has three major components: assess, train, reflect. The first step is to *assess*, that is, decide what you want to improve. For example, you have probably heard that an imperative element for good leadership is being able to provide feedback. Start by breaking down the feedback process into its various aspects—it must be specific, timely, relevant, goal oriented, future focused, and directed at the process, not the person. After you consider these aspects, decide which one you want to improve and *train* on that one alone. Once you get that part down, as determined through *self-reflection*, then move to the area you believe you need to improve next, and so on.

Getting better at anything requires persistence (a.k.a. deliberate practice), as it won't happen overnight. It takes time to become an expert, but we all have what it takes to get started.

THE CHOICE IS YOURS

The best way to adapt and thrive is to know your options and follow the path of least resistance. A complicated problem doesn't need a complicated solution. It needs one that works, and you're more likely to find the right solution if you have options rather than relying on the same approach. A popular saying often attributed to Albert Einstein is, "Insanity is doing the same thing over and over and expecting different results."

Think of a plant growing up through concrete. The plant

---

[44] K. Anders Ericsson, Michael J. Prietula, and Edward T. Cokley, "The Making of an Expert," *Harvard Business Review*, July–August 2007, https://hbr.org/2007/07/the-making-of-an-expert.

didn't break the concrete. It simply found a crack, the path of least resistance. That's resilience. It's about figuring out where the cracks are, what the lowest hanging fruit is, and which option provides the simplest solution so you can start moving forward.

We all have preferred learning styles. Some people learn by reading books and articles, others by listening to podcasts and audiobooks, others by watching documentaries and TED Talks. Some people need time to reflect on what they read or hear or watch, while others are doers who try out what they learn to see how it works. Then there are observers, who want to see others doing the task before they jump in. One isn't better than another, but it is important that we understand ourselves and how we learn. The more we understand and exercise our preferred style, the easier it is to absorb content and grow—another way to follow the path of least resistance.

TAKE ACTION

As I've said before, no matter what your situation, you already have what you need to take the first step. Despite that, most of us find excuses not to get started: "I don't have time," "I don't have the skills," "I'm not ready," "The gym isn't open when I am free," "My boss doesn't trust me," "I don't have money." Ironically, excuses are often valid reasons, but they should not stop you if you are committed to changing your situation. If you can simply take the first step, you create momentum, and once a body is in motion, it will remain in motion.

Using the following strategies, you can raise your standards, make choices, and move forward.

PACE YOURSELF

As discussed in Chapter 4, creating winning habits is key to taking steps toward your aspirational goal. Pick the low-hanging fruit, something you can do right now. Small wins are the key to creating momentum.

As discussed earlier, pacing is one of the three things that will allow you to complete any race, along with nutrition and taking care of your feet. It's important to take the time to learn, reflect, and weigh your options. Some leaders think going fast will bring faster rewards, but this isn't always true. Remember: speed and velocity are not the same. Sometimes we need to slow down and see things from a different angle in order to reach our goals. According to one study of 343 companies, businesses that have the "go, go, go" approach end up with lower sales and operating profits than those that paused to make sure they were working on the most important stuff.[45]

You are stronger than you think, but you also have to pace yourself. Take slow, steady steps to increase your scope or scale your skills or achieve that promotion. Slowing down gives you the opportunity to actively listen, take in different perspectives, build deeper connections, and use the conversations to gain a deeper understanding of the challenge and potential solutions.

You probably are thinking, *I have a million things to do. I don't have time to slow down. I need to get done fast.* I understand this thinking, as I found myself caught in that mindset after my first surgery. I wanted to go back to work fast. I wanted to resume my life where I left it off. Then I realized

---

[45] Jocelyn R. Davis and Tom Atkinson, "Need Speed? Slow Down," *Harvard Business Review*, May 2010, https://hbr.org/2010/05/need-speed-slow-down.

that the only thing I could control was the pace of my recovery, so I started approaching it one step at a time.

Dorie Clark, in her book *The Long Game*, advises entrepreneurs to create space for thinking. She invites us to stop for a moment and ask ourselves if we are trapped in a short-term mindset, working hard but not moving forward. If we are going to be resilient about achieving our aspirational goals, we need to make space for reflection and ask ourselves, "Is this taking me closer to my goal?"

INCREASE STAMINA THROUGH EMPOWERING RITUALS

While attaining those little wins is important, you'll burn out if you don't incorporate "feel good" practices, or empowering rituals, to increase your motivation and stamina. In her book *SuperBetter*, Jane McGonigal writes of her experience recovering from a traumatic head injury. She works as a game designer and decided to use her expertise to get better. In her book, she explains several ways by which we can increase our resilience by controlling our attention, and therefore our thoughts and feelings. To this end, as part of her super better method, McGonigal recommends seven steps to gamify your life and simultaneously increase your stamina.

1. Challenge yourself.
2. Collect and activate powerups.
3. Find and battle the bad guys.
4. Seek out and complete quests.
5. Recruit your allies.
6. Adopt a secret identity.
7. Go for an epic win.

Some of you may remember Super Mario Brothers, the 1980s video game where the hero engaged in an ongoing quest to save the princess During the epic battles toward his quest, Mario encountered little mushrooms, or powerups. If he ate the mushrooms, he became energized. He ran faster and jumped higher and continued his quest with renewed vigor.

Every day we face our own epic battles, and like Mario, we need powerups to keep us going. Your epic battle might be having an uncomfortable conversation or trying to remain upbeat and focused despite your toxic boss. To keep up your stamina for these often taxing quests, you need to recharge.

I have several empowering rituals, or powerups, that recharge me. A powerup is something quick and easy you can do to feel better or to get stronger. Whenever you need a positive emotion or energy, activate a powerup. For example, I start each day with a tall glass of water with lemon and salt to replace the sweat and water lost during the night. Every afternoon, I recharge with a run. At night, I set my intentions for the next day and celebrate the wins of the day. I identify the battles I will face the next day, so that's one less thing to think about first thing in the morning.

In the Super Mario Brothers game, there are turtles whose sole mission is to knock Mario out of the game; those are the enemies he needs to avoid or defeat. The bad guys are anything that makes it harder for you to get stronger and reach your epic win. For me, sugar is one of those enemies, as is the black hole that is social media, so I make a conscious choice to win those battles every day by avoiding cookies and reducing time on social media.

Kimberly, my client who was working on controlling her emotions, lived on the verge of stress overload. She was overworked, stressed, and emotionally drained. As part of the new boundaries she created, she started delegating more to give herself room to breathe and recharge. She also worked on limiting her daily battles to the ones that were truly hers to fight.

On the other side, Kimberly looked for ways to power up so she had enough energy to keep going. To that end, she started mentoring other women in the company who were dealing with similar issues. Even though the group took time from her already busy schedule, meeting with those women empowered Kimberly and increased her motivation at work.

What are your powerups? What empowering rituals give you joy, fill you with peace, and motivate you to keep going when the battle gets tough? What turtles do you need to avoid? Be intentional in your quest to figure it out and take action.

FOCUS ON THE NEXT STEP

If we focus solely on the big moonshot goal, it's easy to become paralyzed and not do anything. This is why I've emphasized focusing on one step at a time.

My wife and I recently decided to replace my son's bicycle. After a few months with no new bike, my wife asked why I hadn't acted on this simple task.

"I don't know what size bike he needs," I replied.

As I thought about it more, I realized I didn't know what size to buy because I hadn't measured his inseam, and I hadn't done that because I didn't have a measuring tape. The silliness of the situation hit me: the first step in this bicycle purchase saga was to get a measuring tape.

My clients often get into the same situation: they focus on the big goal or decision, when all they need to do is figure out the first, often very small, step they need to take.

That said, moving forward one step at a time should not be

confused with doing less than you can achieve. Push yourself a little at a time so that you don't become overwhelmed—but do push yourself. Those small steps should each expand your comfort zone and increase your inner strength, and most importantly, they will allow you to execute on your big-picture game.

EXPERIMENT, REFLECT, PIVOT

When I started my coaching practice, one of my first steps was to find clients and then secure engagements. The first meeting in most potential coaching engagements is the "chemistry meeting," where the prospective client and I get to know each other, explore synergies, and potentially make a decision about working together.

Sometime after my first year in the business, I started an experiment. I began following up with each person, regardless of whether or not the person chose me as a coach. If they selected me, the first question I would ask in our initial formal coaching meeting was "Why did you select me?" If they didn't select me, I sent a follow-up email to ask why.

Using this feedback, I started experimenting with different approaches and ways of conducting these chemistry meetings. Afterward I would reflect on how it went and consider how it might have changed if I had done things differently. Based on this data, I would pivot as needed in my next chemistry meeting with a prospective client. After a few years of data collection, I have developed a chemistry meeting process that works for me. The end result is that I have become more and more successful at landing clients during those initial meetings.

This habit of experimenting, reflecting, and pivoting is key to building resilience and achieving transformational change. After you start taking steps, creating habits, identifying and focusing on daily quests, and using empowering rituals to increase resilience, take time to reflect on your progress. At the end of each quest, ask yourself:

- How did it go?
- What could I have done differently?
- Did I get the result I wanted?
- Will I get the same result if I do this again, or do I need to adapt in a different way?

Adapting involves a repeated series of experimenting, reflecting, and then pivoting if what you tried didn't have the desired result. Sometimes we see one problem as the biggest nail we need to hit, and we go after it again and again, but the nail doesn't move. Rather than continuing to hit that nail in the same way, ask yourself what else you could do. What are the other options for solving this problem? Sometimes you might even need to go back to the beginning and ask yourself if you're solving the right problem. Is this the right nail to hit? Can I use a different hammer?

Resilient individuals adapt; they are open-minded, willing to self-correct, and willing to examine challenges from new perspectives. We all have what it takes to build resilience, but we need to prepare, take action, be willing to push that comfort zone, and learn to sit with discomfort. Remember: you are stronger than you think you are.

MIND, BODY, SPIRIT

Developing inner strength follows the model of a three-legged stool: mind, body, spirit. If you want the stool to stay upright, you need to develop resilience in all three legs.

Before I became an ultrarunner, triathlons were my thing—and a very expensive thing at that. I admired many top triathletes and I tried to learn from them. Two rivals in particular caught my attention—Dave Scott and Mark Allen—because they dominated triathlons in the 1980s and had the biggest rivalry in the Ironman competition.

At the 1989 World Championships in Hawaii, these two athletes participated in a spectacular duel that became known as the Iron War. For 140.6 grueling miles, Scott and Allen swam, cycled, and ran side by side, shoulder to shoulder, at a world-record pace. In the end, Allen won by fifty-eight seconds, and both men demolished the previous record.

During the previous five times they competed in Hawaii, Mark Allen had prepared very well physically, but he struggled mentally. He had negative thoughts about himself and his ability to beat Scott, and the more he thought about these stories, the more they became a reality:[46]

- He is too strong.
- He will never crack.
- Thirteen miles to go and I am already dying.
- It is only going to get worse.
- I have lost again.
- I don't have what it takes to win this race.
- I will never win this race.

---

46 Matt Fitzgerald, *Iron War: Dave Scott, Mark Allen, and the Greatest Race Ever Run* (Boulder, CO: VeloPress, 2012), 201–02.

Prior to the 1989 race, however, Allen trained his spirit and mind, as well as his body. He visited a shaman and started to change the story he was telling himself. Instead of entertaining negative thoughts during the race, he started thinking:

- How cool is this?
- I am leading Ironman with Dave Scott.
- Win or lose this is an amazing experience.
- I am going to enjoy this moment as best as I can. Yes, I am hurting, but Dave is too, I can still win.
- And if I don't, so be it.
- There is more to life.

These thoughts gave Allen the mental strength to keep up with Scott and eventually pull ahead to win.

In the end, Allen found he was stronger than he thought he was. He discovered the truth that if we see things differently, we will think differently, and then we will act differently. The issue is often not our competence, but our attitude and mindset.

Next we'll talk about solving for fulfillment, the pillar that ties together the other four.

RECAP: FIND YOUR INNER STRENGTH

You are stronger and more capable than you think you are. You also have everything you need to take the very first step toward your goal.

Raise Your Standards

Having a high, lofty target motivates us to take risks, make mistakes, get up, and try again, with the end result being increased resilience and higher performance.

What is your moonshot?

Understand Your Choices

By understanding the problems that are yours to solve and those that are not, you can make choices that will actually move you forward.

What must you let go of to get started?

Take Action

Set your direction and take the first step; you already have what it takes to do it. The only truly impossible journey is the one we never start.

What is the first step you must take to start your journey and get momentum?

Chapter 8

SOLVE FOR FULFILLMENT

Uncover your purpose, and in its pursuit, discover both fulfillment and the indelible mark you weave into the tapestry of the world.

- *Find* your purpose.
- *Live* intentionally according to your values.
- *Recharge* to avoid burnout.

My earliest memory is playing hide and seek with my dad. At that point, he was still driving a truck in my grandparents' business, and he would be gone for two or three days at a time. I was three years old and very attached to my father. Whenever he left, I became sad, so my dad created a game to distract me from his actual departure.

When it came time for him to leave, my dad would say,

"Let's play hide-and-seek." I would close my eyes and he would pretend to hide. Instead of hiding, however, he would walk to his truck and leave to take care of his route. Even though I knew my dad was gone, I kept searching. A couple of days would go by, and I still woke up each morning and checked every room in the house. Looking back, I can see that even at that young age, I had developed a coping strategy. Playing that game was my attempt to see things differently so I could deal with my dad's departure.

When I got older, I did something similar with my younger siblings to help them cope with our meager meals. We would pretend that the fried corn tortillas mixed with our eggs were pieces of ground beef or chicken. My mom even played along with the game and would announce that we were having ground beef, eggs, and tortillas for dinner.

As an adult, when I reinvented myself as an executive coach, I again used a similar technique, this time to help my clients view their challenges in a different light—to view them as opportunities instead of obstacles.

It was only many years later, after watching Simon Sinek's Ted Talk and reading his book *Start with Why*, that I understood what I was doing and why I found it so fulfilling. One of Sinek's points is that we all have a why, a purpose, and it is usually embedded in us by the time we're thirteen or fourteen. In his book, Sinek tells the stories of how great leaders find motivation and inspiration for themselves and others by first understanding and communicating their purpose. As they consciously live in that purpose, they find fulfillment.

As an executive coach, I was looking for an edge so people would hire me, so I took a journey to find my why, with the main intention to improve my business.

After reading Sinek's book, I attempted to uncover my

why on my own, but I ended up engaging a consultant from his organization to help me find it. Lee Prosenjak guided me through the process, which involved telling stories of how I had contributed to others and then looking for the impact that contribution had on their lives. I shared several memories, including the one about me playing hide-and-seek and making up games for my siblings. After we talked for a couple of hours or so, Lee said, "You're very good at changing the way you and others see things."

With this start, we then figured out what impact this action has on myself and others. In the "why" model, your purpose has two components: a contribution and an impact. Sinek provides a simple format to put these two parts together as a why statement:

To _____, so that _____.

The first blank represents our contribution to others, and the second blank represents the impact it has. For me, that looks like this:

To reframe the important moments, so that we can adapt and thrive.

This is my why. It is my superpower. I reframe situations for myself, my clients, my children, my wife—everyone. I gain fulfillment from helping others see differently, so they can think differently, so they can act differently.

Fulfillment is an equation that we can and should solve for every day. Fulfillment is found in learning why you do what you do, in learning that you have a specific contribution to make in this world, and then intentionally choosing to make it.

Solving for fulfillment involves finding your purpose, living intentionally, and recharging on a continual basis. In this chapter, we'll discuss how to go about this and build resilience in the process.

FIND YOUR PURPOSE

Many people think of satisfaction and fulfillment as being one and the same, but there is a distinction. Satisfaction has an external driver. It results from achieving or attaining something: getting a promotion, buying a home, running a marathon. Fulfillment, on the other hand, is internally driven. It's what gives you a reason to get up in the morning, apart from external factors. It's the thing you get so absorbed in and excited about that sometimes you forget to eat.

Some people also equate passion and fulfillment. To me, being passionate about something, whether it's classic cars or saving the butterflies, has an inherently selfish component. Passion has an impact on you and your satisfaction, but there's no contribution to others. We frequently hear that we should follow our passion and the money will follow, we'll feel happier, and work won't feel like work. Some point to people like Steve Jobs as evidence that passion leads to these things.

This sounds very compelling, right? The truth is that it doesn't always work like that. The percentage of people who follow their passion and become incredibly successful is very small. For example, of all the people who move to Los Angeles to follow their passion, 98 percent end up working at a low-paying job in places like Starbucks, rather than acting.[47]

---

[47] Oliver E. Williams, Lucas Lacasa, and Vito Latora, "Quantifying and Predicting Success in Show Business," *Nature Communications*, June 4, 2019, https://www.nature.com/articles/s41467-019-10213-0.

Fulfillment is different. It is something gained as we give. I can trace all the pivotal moments in my life to one individual or two who believed in me, challenged me, helped me gain a new perspective, or gave me a first chance. I want to be that person for as many people as I can. I want to help people reframe how they see things so they can think differently, and make different choices and increase their resilience. That's where I find fulfillment. The powerful thing is that I can express my purpose through coaching, as well as in every other relationship.

Kimberly found fulfillment after she started the mentoring group. As she helped others create boundaries and face the pressures of work, Kimberly gained motivation and increased her own resilience.

Like Kimberly, Richard found fulfillment in helping people at work. In the process of increasing his visibility, Richard started mentoring African American employees to help them advance, and in doing so, he found his contribution. He became more proactive, affecting company policy and asking the right questions, all to help his mentees. He found his purpose, and in the process, he happened to get promoted, too.

When we're in survival mode, we're focused on one thing: surviving. We really don't have the capacity to seek or live out our purpose. We simply want to know what will work to get us through and hopefully out of the current challenge. We're not thinking about other people.

When we move on to adapting, we want more than a temporary coping mechanism. We want to figure out how things work so that we can make the situation less difficult. In that sense, adapting is somewhat selfish because our focus is on the satisfaction we feel when we change.

When we move on to thriving, however, we have the internal space to live out our why because we don't have to spend so much time coping and thinking about ourselves. We are moving forward and handling the situation, and we have the capacity to look for and make a contribution to benefit others. As we do, we are fulfilled and motivated to repeat the cycle of contribution and fulfillment. We are happy with our experience and growth and ability to help others, not just when we achieve a goal for ourselves.

No matter what your hardship, your reaction to it determines how your life story develops. In fact, the challenge itself can become part of your purpose. Solving for fulfillment is in itself a powerup as it recharges you in the midst of your own sucky situation.

Solving for fulfillment means finding purpose in everything we do. When we're living our why, we look for opportunities to exercise what we're good at, what has a positive impact on others, and what simultaneously brings us joy. Authentic fulfillment comes when we contribute to others.

To find your own purpose, look inside. What are you already doing that is making an impact on others? You might also read Simon Sinek's books *Start with Why* and *Find Your Why*. Finding and living your why can truly become a north star that allows you to embrace the suck and grow in resilience.

LIVE INTENTIONALLY

Sometimes we find ourselves spending the entire day on autopilot, not even thinking about most of the things we do. Living intentionally is the opposite of functioning on autopilot. It involves being present and mindful as we make day-to-day choices.

You don't have to find your purpose before you can start

living intentionally. Solving for fulfillment involves finding your purpose, living intentionally, and recharging, but those three components don't necessarily happen in a linear fashion.

VALUE-DRIVEN LIFE

After my first wife and I separated, I remained in the Middle East and continued working. Soon, I found myself with two weeks of vacation time. According to the travel agency, Thailand was a hot-ticket destination, so I bought a ticket and took off two days later.

Since I arrived with no plans, I visited the front desk of my hotel and learned about a Buddhist temple retreat that sounded very appealing. Though I knew the retreat involved silence and meditation, I didn't know that I would be spending *seven days* in complete silence.

With talking off the table, there was nothing else to do but sit, walk, write, meditate, and think. It gave me the perfect setting to reflect on my life, particularly what had gone wrong between me and my first wife, and what I was going to do now.

One thing I realized is that Sara and I never talked about our core values. In fact, I don't think we knew what they were. I decided to figure out mine, and by the end of the seven days, I had them:

1. *I value family*: I grew up with a happy family, brothers and sisters and lots of cousins. I realized that family is very important to me. I particularly wanted a family of my own, and that involved having children.
2. *I value emotional and economic independence*: Independence is nothing more than the power to make choices and the integrity to align those choices with our needs. I didn't

want to be as dependent on anyone, and I didn't want to lose my identity to fit in or be liked.
3. *I value learning*: For me, learning isn't about going to school and earning degrees, but about having a continual hunger to expand our understanding in many areas, including the arts. Simply put, learning involves having a growth mindset.
4. *I value emotional intelligence*: When life throws curve balls, people with emotional intelligence handle them with resilience and boundaries, rarely playing the victim or engaging in a nonproductive conflict.
5. *I value fitness and wellness*: I am an avid runner and endurance athlete. Exercise is a big part of who I am and what I do. It is my outlet, a place where I find peace and space to reflect.

When I returned to the States in 2007, I didn't fully understand what I'd accomplished in Thailand. My divorce from Sara had become final, and I was hurting, still blaming myself for the failure of my marriage. I realized where Sara and I had gone wrong: she didn't share any of my core values.

This realization allowed me to finally let go of the blame I'd carried on my shoulders since our separation. It also prompted me to make myself a promise: I would never again compromise my core values. I didn't know it yet, but in three years, I would meet my future wife, Rujeko, someone who shares every one of my values; we even met in a running group.

As we intentionally live out our values, fulfillment will be a natural outcome. Our values are often reflected in our purpose, so we will be contributing to others as we live out our values. The key is intentionality—deliberately contributing and living our values. That's how we solve for fulfillment.

Like me, Richard thought about his values. They were education, equity, and transparency. Also, like me, he looked for ways to intentionally live those values, particularly in the way he leads and works. To do that, Richard decided to use those three values as a north star for how he manages his team, how he talks about himself, and how he works. The result was benefit for his team and fulfillment for Richard.

CREATE YOUR OWN FEEDBACK LOOP

In my work with executives, I often see a big disconnection between how these leaders think their direct reports view them and how they actually do—and often the true sentiment held by direct reports is not flattering. This disconnect seems to grow the further the employee is removed from the leader.

This disconnect occurs for one simple reason: lack of feedback. On the one hand, the higher someone climbs in an organization, the fewer sources of honest feedback they have, partly because direct reports and other stakeholders have conflicting priorities and are afraid to provide direct feedback. In addition, many executives do not actively seek feedback. They simply believe what they are told. As a result, what top executives think of themselves often differs greatly from what everyone else thinks.

When I present 360 interview feedback to my coachees, some find the results shocking. Some are surprised but want to do something about it. Others are surprised and become defensive. Those in the latter group tend to want to justify the results in one of three ways—sometimes all three:

1. *They question the raters*: "They are here to get me." "I have asked them for feedback, and they never told me this." "They are lying."

2. *They question the process/questions*: "The questions are not clear." "The process is flawed." "It is not statistically true."
3. *They question the coach*: "You didn't ask the right questions." "You are a spy." (True story: I was once accused of being a spy to collect dirt about the executive so he could be fired.)

Whether they receive fantastic or horrible feedback, in most cases, it is a defining moment in which clients realize how people see them and either feel good about the comments or see the need to change. That feedback either validates what they're thinking or illuminates their blind spots.

If people at the top only hear positive feedback, they naturally think they're doing great, but the reality might be quite different.

As mentioned in Chapter 5, studies show that ethnic groups who thrive when they immigrate to the United States generally have three qualities in common: they have a sense of superiority, they have a sense of insecurity, and they are relentless about achieving their goals and getting feedback.

Leaders would do well to follow this example. They must know what they bring to the table, and also have a sense of insecurity that causes them to ask, "Am I doing the right thing? Is this the right decision?" These two qualities provide a check and balance.

Likewise, they must seek feedback from others to validate their decisions and to understand the impact of their behavior on others. We all have a certain perspective of our choices or the way we act, and that perspective can be skewed for many reasons. One solution is to generate a feedback loop through a mental model I refer to as *triangulating*.

Astronomers track bodies in space through triangulations.

They look for three stars and then try to determine how the body in question is positioned in relation to those three other celestial objects.

With feedback, triangulating means seeking input from different angles to see where our perspective fits in relation to those other perspectives—especially those that directly oppose our own. If we only ask for feedback from people who reliably agree with our outlook, we miss an opportunity to find out if we are really making the right decisions, handling conflicts in a productive way, and so on. If we ask people who are not usually fond of our decisions or have opposing views, we will likely receive feedback that helps us view the situation from a different angle.

As when you're building resilience in other areas, intentionality is key. Don't pick random people to be part of your feedback loop. If you want to know how you are perceived by direct reports or how your decisions are affecting those you lead, ask your direct reports and those you lead, as well as an outside observer like your manager.

A leader at the top who only receives one opinion is like a judge hearing a legal case and only hearing the prosecution's view or the defense attorney's view. One cannot make a fair or accurate decision based on one side of the story.

Keep in mind that whatever decision you make, it's only one of several options. If you find yourself thinking you have only two options—yes or no, this or that—seek out more feedback. There are likely many options beyond this or that, but you may have to actively look for them. When clients come to me thinking there are only two options in a particular situation, I sometimes use the vanishing option test, which I learned from *Decisive* by Chip and Dan Heath. For example, a client told me, "I have this particular employee who is not performing, and I am deciding if he should stay or go."

"Imagine that firing him is *not* an option," I replied. "Then what else could you do?"

He thought for a moment and then started sharing other options, one of which he eventually chose.

Remember, influence rule number one is to be open to being influenced. When you seek feedback from people who think differently and have different opinions, you are following this rule. You show vulnerability and increase your level of influence tenfold if you approach someone and say something like "I've been thinking about X. You usually give me strong feedback about my decision, so what do you think about X?"

Creating a feedback loop shows a growth mindset. In asking for comments and suggestions, especially from those with opposing views, you're essentially asking for ways to adapt and thrive, which is the essence of resilience.

RECHARGE

When we are faced with changes and challenges, and we are in survival mode, it's easy to become stressed and overwhelmed, sometimes to the point of complete burnout. Even if we are consciously building our resilience muscle by embracing the suck and loving our life, it is possible to become burned out.

Whatever the cause of stress or overwhelm, the solution is the same: recharge. One way to recharge and help others at the same time is to solve for fulfillment and live intentionally.

For example, Kimberly is a giver. She was overwhelmed and stressed because she wasn't creating boundaries, which caused her to overstretch herself and her team, which in turn caused her to be defensive and difficult to work with. Then she started the women's group to help them learn the lessons she had. That is now her source of recharging. She feels appreciated. She gets fulfillment not only from the actual mentoring, but from the feedback she receives from the women she's helping. The irony is that instead of doing less, she actually took on more. But the group work served as a recharge mechanism for her depleted emotional tank.

The unintended consequence is that Kimberly has affected how these women show up to work, which is impacting the organization as a whole, and her influence hasn't gone unnoticed. When the company recently went through a reorganization, Kimberly was tapped to head one of the most complex and important business units. Two years ago, she was on the brink of resigning and people couldn't handle working with her. Now she is adding tremendous value to the organization because she is being fulfilled; she's no longer feeling drained, which is the main outcome of being overwhelmed.

In keeping his door open and solving problems for everyone who showed up, Jake felt useful—and used. That open-door policy created a great deal of stress for him. People depended on him, and he put himself in a position to solve the problems for them. Some of those problems were grievances about interpersonal dynamics, not just about the work being done. People expected Jake to have an answer to their problems and he thought it was his job to provide one, all the time. But the pressure of having to come up with a solution to every problem became too much. Jake's passion was no longer bringing him fulfillment. In the fulfillment cycle, when we're living out our purpose, we should be enjoying a reward along with the contribution we're making to others. Jake needed to find a different way of helping people, one that didn't leave him drained.

Jake and I worked on how to close that loop. Rather than solving problems for those who come to him, Jake has now started helping people see how they can find purpose, align the dots, and, most importantly, solve their own problems. He became a leader coach, so the burden is on the individuals to do the work, but Jake contributes to their success and he is recharged by seeing people connect the dots and find purpose.

Everyone recharges in different ways. The key is to find what works for you. Chances are that intentionally living out your values and purpose will fill your love tank and give you the powerup you need to keep going.

THE KEYSTONE PILLAR

Living a meaningful life goes beyond the pursuit of happiness or satisfaction. It is also linked to resilience. One study showed that people with purpose show better emotional recovery following a negative experience. They are also more inclined to be positive and less likely to ruminate, and therefore, are less prone to stress.[48]

Having a purpose makes it easier to commit to an outcome, persist through hardship, and be optimistic about the future. It is much harder to give up when you have a purpose. Above all, people living with a purpose are able to find meaning and learning in all of life's experiences, both good and bad.

Solving for fulfillment is the pillar that ties the other four together. It's the keystone of resilience. If you find your purpose and intentionally live a value-driven life, you will find it easier to embrace the suck, face your fears, build relationships, and find your inner strength. You will be better able to

---

[48] Stacey M. Schaefer et al., "Purpose in Life Predicts Better Emotional Recovery from Negative Stimuli," *PLoS ONE* 8, no. 11, https://journals.plos.org/plosone/article?id=10.1371/journal.pone.0080329.

withstand suffering and discomfort, knowing that doing so is leading toward a greater purpose.

In addition, there is a definite business case for finding and executing your purpose. As Kimberly and Richard and so many others have found, if you look for opportunities to live your purpose within your organization, the unintended consequences will be incredibly positive for yourself and others.

RECAP: SOLVE FOR FULFILLMENT

You find fulfillment in learning why you do what you do, in learning that you have a specific contribution to make in this world, and in intentionally choosing to make it.

Find Your Purpose

Your purpose has a contribution and an impact, and you probably are doing it already.

What have you been consistently doing (your contribution) that is making a positive impact on others and makes you forget to eat?

Live Intentionally

Resilience and success are not an accident. They result from the choices we make every day.

What do you do every day that aligns with your purpose?

Recharge

Everyone recharges in different ways. The key is to find what works for you.

When do you feel the most energized and motivated?

CONCLUSION

Life is complex, but it doesn't require complex solutions. In fact, we can actively reduce its complexity and make it more predictable by figuring out what we can control and taking steps to do so. No matter what difficulties life brings, we have the power to make decisions that will move us past surviving to adapt and thrive.

When faced with challenges—whether a brain tumor, being passed over for a promotion, or overcoming our fears—we can choose to give up and play the victim. We can choose to blame others. We can choose to play it safe. Or we can choose to exercise commitment, persistence, and optimism. We can choose to love our fate, embrace the suck, and take the first step toward transformation. We can choose to tap into what we already have day by day, and eventually make ordinary resilience part of our thriving mechanism.

Yes, it takes a lot of self-compassion to move past our last mistake. It requires courage to feel fear and act anyway. It takes discipline to make it happen in the long run. But we already have what we need to take the first step.

START WHERE YOU ARE

When I started writing this book, I didn't know how it would turn out. I simply knew I had something to say, so I started writing it. No matter what you want to accomplish, no matter what issue you want to overcome—you can. You just need to take the first step.

My goal is to help you build resilience to navigate a current crisis, but even more, I want to show you how to intentionally build resilience when life is good so you're ready for the next challenge, however traumatic or mundane.

To that end, start where you are right now:

- What winning habits can you create to develop physical, mental, spiritual, or social resilience?
- What relationships can you intentionally start building?
- What longstanding fears can you challenge?
- What personal standards can you raise to increase your performance?
- What mini resilience challenges can you consciously create to exercise your ability to adapt and push out the boundaries of your comfort zone?

Remember, resilience is a dish better served cold. The more you can do when you're not in crisis, the better prepared you'll be when you are.

If you are currently in the midst of a hardship, the answer is the same: start where you are. After all, the struggle you are in today is simply developing the strength you will need for the future.

- Figure out what you are dealing with. What are the challenges? Which problems are truly yours to solve?

- Figure out your aspirational goal. Where do you see yourself in the future? Use that vision as a north star.
- Figure out your first step. Which direction are you going to start walking in? What is one small, safe step you can take in that direction?

Then rinse, wash, and repeat. No matter what complexities come your way, the framework for dealing with them is always the same: reframe what you see, so you can change how you think, so you can transform how you act.

The goal of resilience is not "I am okay with this, I'll survive."

The goal is not "I feel good about this. It will be okay. I'll adapt."

The goal is to love your fate, *amor fati*, to be able to say, "I feel great about this. It was meant to happen. I am going to make the best of it. I will thrive."

Given that goal, ask yourself this: what is one thing you can do today so that three years from now you can confidently say that your current crisis is the best thing that happened to your career/company/life? Then do it.

FOR YOURSELF AND OTHERS

Although resilience does have a self-preservation aspect, it is also something you do for others. As a leader, mother, father, spouse, or friend, the resilience you build is not only for yourself; it's also for your clients, coworkers, spouse, children, and anyone else who crosses your path.

I am working on my resilience so I can help my daughter and son become resilient so they can adapt and thrive no matter what comes their way.

I am married to an African American woman. I am also a

person of color, but if I don't open my mouth and reveal my accent, I could pass as white. Not so for my wife and children. Shortly after George Floyd's death in May 2020, my daughter asked, "Daddy, if the police come, are they going to kill me?" My six-year-old shouldn't have to ask that question. With the current state of the world, I am afraid for my children, that they will be judged and treated harshly because of the color of their skin. I feel sad that they don't have the luxury of "passing" like I do.

I cannot change police brutality. I cannot change the widespread racism or inequality. Those are problems that are not mine to solve alone. However, I have seen and experienced firsthand how people of color, my wife included, are ignored, discounted, and dismissed. That's a problem I can take steps to solve, at least in my immediate sphere of influence. I can make room for myself, my family, and others. I can acknowledge every person of color I encounter so we do not feel invisible.

Immediately after the killing of George Floyd, I realized that many people were not comfortable talking about it, because they didn't know what to say or how to say it. So they remained silent. I decided to provide a safe space for them to talk about it, if they chose to. My goal was not to persuade them to think a certain way, but to provide a safe space to express their feelings about the issue. I made the uncomfortable moment a little more comfortable. This is my way of adding a little resilience to the world.

Similarly, the principles in this book are meant to help you reframe challenges so you can become a resilient leader. But that's not where it stops. Like Kimberly and Richard, you can take what you've learned and help others develop their own resilience, whether it's people on your team or your children.

What can you do to build resilience, to elevate others, to

live your values, and to make your contribution to the world? Companies and societies become resilient due to the additive value of resilient people working in that company and residing in that society. It's been said that if you want to master something, teach it to somebody else. As you do, you are not just helping people to become resilient, you strengthen your resilience as well.

People build resilience faster if the environment allows it, and it's your responsibility as a leader to provide that safe space. Leaders who inspire, who want others to grow, who are inclusive, and who provide honest feedback and seek the same from others will build their own resilience and encourage the same in others.

As I finish this book, people are still experiencing the impact of COVID-19, personally and professionally. In addition to the lost lives, the economic damage is significant and has touched people around the globe.

In a personal, societal, organizational crisis such as the one brought on by COVID-19, the lessons from this book are relevant. To embrace the suck and combat fears, we must remain optimistic about the future, committed to moving forward, and persistent despite the struggles. As each of us uses this opportunity to build personal resilience, we will also become more resilient as a society.

As a member of the human race, I hope you take the lessons from this book to build resilience for yourself, and in so doing, make the world a better place. If we all become more intentional about adapting and thriving ourselves, things will start changing in the right direction for everyone. When we flex our resilient muscles, we learn how to embrace the beautiful beings that we are.

I would love to know what you think about this book

or if I can help in any way. Please drop me a note at luis@ordinaryresilience.com.

Now go out there and break things.

ACKNOWLEDGMENTS

To my parents, who brought me to this world, which alone is the biggest gift ever. You raised me to be strong and confident, despite the limitations. You didn't have much, but your resilience has been a source of inspiration and has made a positive impact in my life. You showed me that I can make lemonade out of anything that resembles a lemon, and how to stretch a dollar in ways I still cannot comprehend.

To my brothers and sisters, for whom I am very grateful. Resilience runs in the family. I see how much you have grown professionally and personally, and the best thing of all, you all are incredibly kind and compassionate. Mary, Jose, Oscar, and Rosa Maria, you have been a source of inspiration—and the reason why I left home so early (just kidding).

To my beautiful wife, Rujeko, who changed the course of my life and has been the most important bastion of support in my entrepreneurial journey. You are kind and compassionate; I still cannot believe how I got so lucky. I thought I spent all of my luck when I survived the tumor. You could have done so much better! We might not agree on everything, especially who is the better cook, but we agree on what is important, and that is what matters.

To my two beautiful children, Alexis and Nathan, who have given new meaning to my life, while simultaneously testing my patience. Without you, this book could have been written two years earlier. And I love you anyway!

And to you, holding this book. Can you put your hand on the page and imagine I am giving you a high five? How else do I thank you for reading my book, and for the Amazon review you are going to write?

ABOUT THE AUTHOR

LUIS VELASQUEZ is a leadership coach in Silicon Valley and a facilitator for the Stanford Graduate School of Business. He was raised in the middle of a civil war and is a brain tumor warrior. Once a university professor and research scientist, he now helps leaders learn, grow, and change by showing them how to reframe their challenges and take the most beneficial next step. Mid-level managers to C-suite executives from around the world hire Luis and Velas Coaching to help them unlock their own resilience, adapt, and thrive. For more information about Luis and Velas Coaching, visit www.velascoaching.com.

www.ingramcontent.com/pod-product-compliance
Lightning Source LLC
Chambersburg PA
CBHW030442090526
44586CB00044B/553